With Stories Learning English

cemal yazıcı

Published by cemal yazıcı, 2024.

While every precaution has been taken in the preparation of this book, the publisher assumes no responsibility for errors or omissions, or for damages resulting from the use of the information contained herein.

WITH STORIES LEARNING ENGLISH

First edition. November 24, 2024.

Copyright © 2024 cemal yazıcı.

ISBN: 979-8227387967

Written by cemal yazıcı.

With Stories

LEARNING ENGLISH

PREFACE

Our collection of "Easy and Challenged Stories" is the perfect companion to improving your language. Whether you are a beginner or an advanced learner, these stories are perfect for you.
While you are learning the basics of the language, you can also increase your vocabulary with the stories you read. These short stories dealing with situations you may encounter in daily life will help you expand your vocabulary and improve your logical storage.
There are simple and enjoyable stories for beginner language learners, as well as challenging stories that offer deep meanings and a rich vocabulary for more advanced English language learners. These outstanding stories offer the perfect opportunity to expand your narrative and become familiar with complex sentence structures.
This storybook will not only improve your reading but also your ability to think and understand English.

TWO GIRLS IN PARIS.

OUR CLASS LEARNS ENGLISH.

A BOY AN UMBRELLA AND THE JOURNEY TO SCHOOL

A STORY OF RESILIENCE AND WISDOM

A LITTLE BOY'S ADVENTURE.

A STORY OF FRIENDSHIP AMONG GIRLS.

THE POWER OF STORYTELLING

A YOUNG COUPLE'S PARISIAN ADVENTURE

CEMAL YAZICI

With Stories

LEARNING ENGLISH

ENGLISH BETWEEN LINES

Stories prepared in short and understandable terms; It is easy to read, entertaining, and with the lesson learned from the story section at the end of each story, it makes it easier for you to have a better grasp of the story you are reading. The fact that you can sometimes find advice on learning a language offers you more than just a storybook.

ENGLISH DIALOGUE DIARIES 1-2

"Unlock the joy of learning English with our engaging two-book set!

Dive into fun, interactive dialogues that make mastering the language enjoyable and effective. Perfect for learners of all levels, this collection enhances your conversational skills while keeping the process entertaining.

Start your English learning adventure today!"

PREFACE

With Stories Learning English

Our collection of "Easy and Challenged Stories" is the perfect companion to improving your language. Whether you are a beginner or an advanced learner, these stories are perfect for you.

While you are learning the basics of the language, you can also increase your vocabulary with the stories you read. These short stories dealing with situations you may encounter in daily life will help you expand your vocabulary and improve your logical storage.

There are simple and enjoyable stories for beginner language learners, as well as challenging stories that offer deep meanings and a rich vocabulary for more advanced English language learners. These outstanding stories offer the perfect opportunity to expand your narrative and become familiar with complex sentence structures.

This storybook will not only improve your reading but also your ability to think and understand English.

While every precaution has been taken in the preparation of this book, the publisher assumes no responsibility for errors or omissions, or for damages resulting from the use of the information contained herein.

WITH STORIES LEARNING ENGLISH
First edition. November 24, 2024.
Copyright © 2024 cemal yazıcı.
Written by cemal yazıcı.

A little boy's adventure

With Stories

LEARNING ENGLISH

A LITTLE BOY'S ADVENTURE

As the sun began to rise over the horizon, casting a warm golden glow across the landscape, six-year-old Ethan was beyond excited. This weekend marked a special adventure for him: a trip to his grandparents' farm. Living in the bustling city with its concrete jungles and busy streets, Ethan had always cherished his visits to the countryside, where the air was fresh, the sounds of nature were abundant, and adventure awaited at every corner.

The journey to the farm felt like an eternity. Buckled snugly in the backseat of his parents' car, Ethan gazed out the window, watching as the city skyline faded into distant buildings and sprawling green fields began to unfold before his eyes. With each passing mile, his excitement grew—he could already picture the barn, the animals, and the endless possibilities that awaited him.

Upon arrival, Ethan was greeted with open arms by his grandparents, who wore smiles as warm as the sunshine that illuminated the farm. His grandmother swept him into a tight embrace, her floral apron flapping in the breeze, while his grandfather stood nearby, tipping his straw hat in greeting. "Ready for some adventure?" Grandpa asked, his eyes twinkling with mischief.

Ethan's heart raced at the thought of exploring. After quickly unloading the car, he dashed toward the sprawling fields. His first stop was the barn, where he was greeted by a chorus of mooing cows and clucking chickens. The barn was a treasure trove of sights and sounds—hay bales stacked high, old farming tools hanging on the walls, and the sweet scent of animals mingling in the air.

"Can I help feed the animals?" Ethan asked, eyes wide with anticipation.

"Absolutely!" his grandfather replied, leading him to a stall where the cows were munching on fresh hay. With careful guidance and a bucket filled with feed, Ethan learned the delicate art of feeding the gentle giants. He laughed as one curious cow nudged his arm, begging for more food, and he reached out hesitantly to pet its soft, velvety nose.

After helping with the cows, Ethan couldn't resist the calls of the playful pigs in the nearby pen. With his grandpa's assurance, he ventured into the pen, careful of the muddy ground. The pigs rolled around, splashing mud everywhere, and Ethan soon found himself laughing uncontrollably as they snorted and grunted around him. "This is the best!" he exclaimed, his voice bubbling with joy.

With Stories

LEARNING ENGLISH

A LITTLE BOY'S ADVENTURE

As the afternoon sun began to dip lower in the sky, casting long shadows across the fields, it was time for a classic farm tradition: apple picking. His grandmother led him to the orchard, where branches were heavy with ripe, red apples. "Let's see how many we can pick!" she said. As they filled their basket, Ethan learned to carefully twist the apples to pick them without damaging the trees. He relished munching on sun-warmed apples, their sweet juice dripping down his chin.

That evening, after a hearty farm-style dinner prepared by his grandma, Ethan and his family gathered around a crackling fire outside. They roasted marshmallows for s'mores, and Ethan shared stories from his school, while his grandparents told him tales of their younger days on the farm. The stars twinkled like diamonds in the night sky, and Ethan felt an overwhelming sense of happiness and belonging.

When it was time to head to bed, he crept into the cozy guest room in the farmhouse. With the soothing sounds of crickets outside and the faint rustle of the wind through the trees, Ethan closed his eyes, dreaming of all the adventures still to come. He imagined riding on a tractor, searching for hidden eggs in the chicken coop, and maybe even helping his grandpa fix a fence.

The weekend on the farm was a magical escape from the fast-paced life of the city. For Ethan, it was not just about the animals or the apple picking; it was about the memories created, the laughter shared, and the love of family that wrapped around him like a warm blanket. As the sun would rise again the next day, Ethan couldn't wait to embrace more of the joys that life on the farm had to offer. It was a precious time that he would cherish forever, and he knew he would count the days until he could return again.

A story of friendship among girls

With Stories

LEARNING ENGLISH

A STORY OF FRIENDSHIP AMONG GIRLS

In a world where digital screens dominate our lives, the magic of cinema retains an unparalleled charm, especially among groups of friends. The experience of watching a movie unfolds a beautiful narrative, one that goes beyond the screen to weave stories of friendship, laughter, and shared experiences. This is particularly true for a group of girls who found joy, solace, and adventure nestled in the darkened corners of their local cinema.

A Sunday Tradition

Every Sunday, five girls—Emma, Mia, Sara, Lily, and Zoe—gather at the local cinema to watch the latest releases. For them, this ritual isn't just about the films; it's about the time spent together, creating memories that would last a lifetime. Their friendship blossomed in high school and has only strengthened each week through shared popcorn, whispered commentary, and heart-felt discussions during the credits.

The Anticipation

With each new release, the excitement builds. Whether it's a romantic comedy, an action-packed thriller, or a heartwarming animated feature, the girls passionately discuss their expectations. They often hypothesize about plots and characters, creating their own narratives long before the film begins. This anticipation is a part of the fun—an engaging precursor to the cinematic journey they are about to embark on.

With Stories
LEARNING ENGLISH

A STORY OF FRIENDSHIP AMONG GIRLS

The Cinematic Experience

As the lights dim and the screen comes alive, the outside world fades away. The girls immerse themselves in the story being told—laughing at comedic moments, gasping at surprising twists, and wiping away tears during emotional scenes. It's a beautifully shared experience, where reactions are instinctive and unfiltered. They exchange glances, laughter, or an occasional squeeze of the hand during nail-biting moments, reinforcing the bond they share.

One Sunday, they decided to watch a coming-of-age film that resonated with their own experiences. They laughed at the awkwardness of adolescence and reflected on their own journeys through life. Afterwards, they found themselves discussing the themes of the movie long into the night, sharing their dreams and fears, and realizing how the story mirrored their lives.

Bonds Strengthened By Stories

Cinema has this incredible power to evoke emotions, spark conversations, and deepen relationships. As the credits rolled, each girl felt empowered by the narratives they witnessed. They left the theater not only entertained but feeling understood and inspired. Discussions about character arcs and moral dilemmas often paved the way for sharing their own stories, showcasing their vulnerabilities and dreams.

A particularly memorable film—a thrilling adventure—left them buzzing with excitement. They spent hours afterward imagining themselves as the heroines of the story, devising plans for their own adventures in the summer ahead, dreaming big, and believing that anything was possible.

With Stories
LEARNING ENGLISH

A STORY OF FRIENDSHIP AMONG GIRLS

The Cinematic Experience

Reflecting on Their Love for Cinema
The girls' love for cinema also expanded beyond the theater. They started creating their own movie nights at home, discussing classic films, and even exploring the art of filmmaking through short projects. They bonded over their shared love for storytelling, learning not just about movies but also about each other. Every film ignited new passions, prompting them to pursue creative outlets like writing, poetry, and acting.

Conclusion: More Than Just Movies
The story of these five girls is one of friendship, growth, and the enriching power of cinema. Each visit to the cinema allowed them to escape reality, explore new perspectives, and celebrate life together. For them, it was never just about watching a movie; it was about experiencing life to the fullest, nurturing their bond, and creating cherished memories.
In an age where technology often pulls us apart, the cinema has the unique ability to bring people together—reminding us that, sometimes, the best stories are lived, shared, and remembered together. The joy these girls found in the cinema is a testament to the timeless magic of films and the irreplaceable connections they foster.

With Stories
LEARNING ENGLISH

"Discover our curated collection of **English stories** books designed to enhance your language skills!
Catering to various levels, from beginner to advanced, these engaging tales provide an enjoyable way to improve vocabulary, comprehension, and fluency.
Dive into captivating narratives and watch your English proficiency soar!" Perfect for people of all ages, this book makes the journey to fluency enjoyable and effective with its engaging narratives.
Have fun while improving your comprehension and speaking skills!" "Unlock the joy of learning English with captivating storybooks!
Dive into engaging tales that enhance vocabulary, comprehension, and language skills while enjoying the art of storytelling. Perfect for learners of all ages, discover how reading can make mastering English an exciting adventure!"

The English Explorer
Unlock the world of imagination with our captivating collection of English reading stories! Designed for readers of all ages, this anthology is a treasure trove of engaging tales that transport you to realms filled with adventure, romance, and unforgettable characters. Indulge your curiosity as you navigate through diverse narratives that inspire the mind and ignite the spirit of exploration.
Each story is meticulously crafted, offering unique plots that blend excitement and emotion, ensuring there's something for everyone.
From daring quests in enchanted lands to heartwarming tales of love and friendship, every page invites you to lose yourself in a new adventure.
Perfect for cozy evenings or adventurous afternoons, this collection not only entertains but also enhances language skills and fosters a love for reading. Whether you're sharing stories with family or enjoying a solitary escape, these enchanting tales are bound to spark joy and imagination. Join us on this literary journey and discover the magic that lies within the pages. Unleash your imagination and embark on an adventure today!

Two girls in Paris

With Stories

LEARNING ENGLISH

Two Girls in Paris: A Journey of Friendship and Adventure

Paris, the City of Light, has long captivated hearts with its enchanting streets, historic architecture, and the promise of adventure. For two young girls, Emma and Sophie, this dreamy destination was more than just a vacation; it was a chance to weave unforgettable memories and explore the magic that Paris has to offer.
Setting Off on an Adventure
With their backpacks packed and excitement bubbling, Emma and Sophie set off on their journey from their small hometown. The flight buzzed with anticipation; they spent it sharing stories of the adventures they hoped to have, from indulging in delicious pastries to discovering the secrets of charming alleyways. Little did they know, their shared experience would deepen their friendship and leave them with memories they'd cherish forever.

The Eiffel Tower: A Dream Realized
Upon landing, the girls made their way to the iconic Eiffel Tower. Standing beneath its towering structure, they felt as if they had stepped into a postcard. The sun began to set, casting a golden hue over the iron lattice work. They took countless selfies, their laughter echoing around them. As they ascended to the viewing platform, the sprawling cityscape of Paris unfolded before their eyes, and both girls felt a rush of exhilaration. "This is incredible," Emma exclaimed, her eyes wide with wonder. Sophie, unable to contain her joy, twirled around, feeling like she was on top of the world. They promised to make this moment last a lifetime.

With Stories
LEARNING ENGLISH

Two Girls in Paris: A Journey of Friendship and Adventure

A Taste of Paris

No visit to Paris would be complete without indulging in its culinary delights. The girls wandered into a quaint café in Montmartre, where they savored fresh croissants and rich hot chocolate. They learned the importance of taking time to savor their food – a lesson that seemed to resonate in every delightful bite.

Later, they ventured to the famous Rue Cler market, where the vibrant colors of fruits and flowers dazzled their senses. After sampling some cheese and baguettes, they found a sunny spot in the nearby Champ de Mars, where they spread out a picnic blanket. Delicious food and the backdrop of the Eiffel Tower created a perfect scene, blending the charm of Parisian life with the comfort of their friendship.

Intriguing Art and History

The girls knew that their Paris adventure would also be incomplete without a visit to the Louvre. As they marveled at the masterpieces, including the enigmatic smile of the Mona Lisa, they engaged in playful debates about their interpretations of art. The sheer size of the museum was overwhelming, but they navigated the halls together, guiding one another on this cultural journey.

In the heart of the city, they visited the historic Notre-Dame Cathedral, where they marveled at the gothic architecture and the intricate stained glass windows. Here, amidst the crowds, they found a peaceful moment to reflect on their travels, realizing how much they had learned about each other and the world around them.

With Stories
LEARNING ENGLISH

Two Girls in Paris: A Journey of Friendship and Adventure

Experiencing the Romance of Paris

As their trip progressed, Emma and Sophie explored various neighborhood each with its unique charm. They strolled along the Seine River at sunset the bridges illuminated by glowing lanterns, and shared their dreams for t future. Paris, with its romantic ambiance, inspired them to think about th adventures that lay ahead in their lives.

On their last evening, they climbed to Montmartre to watch the sunset ov the city. The breathtaking view was filled with pink and orange hues tha reflected their joy and the bittersweet feeling of an adventure coming to close. They promised to always keep the spirit of Paris in their hearts.

A Friendship Strengthened

As Emma and Sophie boarded their flight back home, they were filled with sense of fulfillment. Their adventure in Paris had strengthened their bon filled with laughter, exploration, and a new appreciation for different cultures. The city had gifted them not only experiences but also memorie that would last a lifetime.

In the years to come, whenever they thought of Paris, they would also thir of each other—two girls who ventured into the unknown together, discovering both the world and themselves in the process. Their Parisian adventure would remain a beautiful chapter in the story of their friendshi inspiring them to embrace new journeys in the future.

Our class learns English

With Stories

LEARNING ENGLISH

Our Class Learns English: A Journey of Discovery

In our bustling classroom, filled with laughter, curiosity, and the occasional debate over the best superhero, a remarkable journey unfolds every day: the journey of learning English. For many of us, English represents a new horizon—an opportunity to connect with the world beyond our walls and to express ourselves in ways we never thought possible.

Our First Steps: The Basics

It all began with the basics. Our teacher, Ms. Johnson, introduced us to the alphabet—the building blocks of our newfound language. With her infectious enthusiasm, she guided us through each letter, turning what could have been a daunting task into an exciting adventure. We sang songs, played games, and even created colorful posters to decorate our classroom walls. Each letter we learned was not just a character; it was a gateway to new words and ideas.

As we progressed, our vocabulary began to flourish. Words that once seemed foreign to us became familiar friends. We learned to describe our world in ways we never imagined, and soon enough, simple sentences began to take shape. "The cat is black," we would proudly declare, as if announcing a great triumph.

With Stories
LEARNING ENGLISH

Exploring Grammar: A New Challenge

With a solid foundation in vocabulary, we turned our attention to grammar. We learned about nouns, verbs, and adjectives. Though it seemed tricky at times, our class soon discovered the rhythm and flow of sentence construction. Ms. Johnson often emphasized that grammar is like the rules of a game; once you understand them, you can play with creativity.

Through engaging activities, we practiced our skills. Whether it was partnering up to write silly stories or working in groups to construct the tallest sentence tower, we embraced every challenge. We learned that it's okay to make mistakes, as they're simply stepping stones on our path to fluency.

Immersing Ourselves in English

As our confidence grew, so did our desire to immerse ourselves in English. To enhance our learning, Ms. Johnson introduced us to a variety of multimedia resources—books, songs, podcasts, and movies. We discovered the joys of reading new stories, feeling our imaginations take flight as characters leaped off the pages.

The class held a 'Media Friday'—a dedicated time each week where we would discuss our favorite English-language shows, songs, or books. We debated over plot twists, analyzed song lyrics, and even acted out short scenes. This immersion made language learning feel less like a chore and more like a vibrant part of our daily lives.

With Stories
LEARNING ENGLISH

Building Connections: Communication is Key

Learning English has also allowed us to connect with each other in ways we hadn't before. As our language skills improved, we began sharing stories from our own cultures, drawing parallels and celebrating our differences. We organized a cultural day where each student presented something unique about their heritage—complete with food, music, and of course, a little English practice.

These moments of connection not only strengthened our friendships but also fostered an appreciation for diversity in our classroom. We realized that while we were learning English, we were also learning about empathy, respect, and collaboration.

Looking Ahead: The Journey Continues

As we wrap up another semester, it's clear that our journey in learning English is far from over. Each lesson has opened up new possibilities, and we can already see the impact it will have on our futures. Whether it's for travel, pursuing further education, or career opportunities, the skills we're acquiring today will serve us well in the years to come.

With Stories
LEARNING ENGLISH

With Ms. Johnson's encouragement, we've set personal goals for ourselves. Some of us aim to read an entire English novel, while others are eager to write letters to pen pals in other countries. The world has become our classroom, and we are excited to take everything we've learned beyond the four walls of our school.

In conclusion, learning English is not just about mastering a language; it's about building confidence, forging connections, and opening doors to new adventures. Each new word we learn, every grammatical rule we master, and all the stories we share are pieces of a larger puzzle.

Together, as a class, we are not just learning English; we are creating a vibrant tapestry of experiences that will influence our lives for years to come.

With Stories Learning English

As we approach the conclusion of yet another semester, it becomes increasingly apparent that our journey in learning English is far from finished. Each lesson we have participated in has opened up a myriad of new possibilities, and the impact of our hard work and dedication is already coming into view as we contemplate our futures. Whether our aspirations include traveling to new and exciting destinations, pursuing advanced education, or seeking out promising career opportunities, the skills we are diligently acquiring today will undoubtedly serve us well in the years ahead.

With the unwavering encouragement and support from Ms. Johnson, we have taken the initiative to set ambitious personal goals for ourselves. For some of us, this means tackling the challenge of reading an entire English novel, immersing ourselves in the world of literature and expanding our vocabulary. Others among us are particularly enthusiastic about the prospect of writing heartfelt letters to pen pals located in far-off countries, forging international friendships that transcend borders and cultures. It is truly inspiring to witness how the world has evolved into our classroom, and we are enthusiastic about the opportunity to apply everything we have learned beyond the confines of our school environment.

In summary, the process of learning English is not limited to merely mastering a language; it encompasses the invaluable experience of building self-confidence, establishing meaningful connections, and unlocking the doors to a multitude of new adventures. Each new word we acquire, every grammatical rule we meticulously master, and all the stories we share with one another represent essential pieces of a larger puzzle. Together, as a cohesive class, we are not only learning English; we are crafting a vibrant tapestry of experiences and memories that will indelibly influence our lives for years to come. The journey is ongoing, and we eagerly anticipate where it will lead us next.

A boy an umbrella and the journey to school

With Stories
LEARNING ENGLISH

A Boy, an Umbrella, and the Journey to School

It was one of those rainy, drizzly mornings that seem to dull the vibrancy of life. The clouds hung low in the sky, casting a muted grayness over the little town of Willowbrook. In a cozy home on Maple Street, a young boy named Lucas prepared for his day. He pulled on his favorite blue raincoat, slipped on his bright yellow rubber boots, and grabbed the one item he knew would be essential—his trusty umbrella.

This wasn't just any umbrella. It was a vivid creation adorned with colorful dinosaurs, a birthday gift from his grandmother. Each time Lucas opened it, he felt the excitement that came with a thrilling adventure, even on the most mundane of days. Today, it would protect him from the drizzling rain that had taken hold of the morning.

As he stepped outside, the familiar aroma of wet earth and fresh rain greeted him. Lucas opened his umbrella, and immediately, the world under its canopy transformed. He felt like he had donned a magical shield, warding off the dreary weather. Each step he took created small splashes in the puddles that dotted the sidewalk, and with the umbrella above him, he felt a sense of empowerment. Nothing could dampen his spirits today!

The route to school was familiar—a short trek down Elm Street and a left at the big oak tree, which stood like a steadfast guardian. Lucas noticed other children huddled under their own umbrellas or darting for cover beneath awnings. Some laughed, while others hurried, eager to escape the drizzle. But Lucas walked at his own pace, twirling the umbrella as if it were a baton, and occasionally pretending it was a spaceship taking him on a journey to distant planets.

With Stories
LEARNING ENGLISH

As he turned the corner, he spotted his friend Mia, who was struggling with her own umbrella. The gusty wind had given her trouble, flipping it inside out just as she was about to cross the road. Without hesitation, Lucas rushed over to help. They laughed together as they fixed Mia's umbrella, each feeling the warmth of friendship shine brighter than the cloudy skies above.

With both umbrellas now in working order, the duo continued toward school, chatting about everything from their favorite dinosaurs to the latest episode of their favorite cartoon. The rain became a backdrop to their laughter and excitement, reinforcing the bond they shared. Lucas realized that while the weather may seem gloomy, it brought unexpected joy—a chance to connect and create memories.

Upon arriving at school, Lucas and Mia stood in front of the tall brick building, still smiling. They gave each other a fist bump, their hearts filled with the kind of happiness only found in shared moments. The rain began to lighten as they walked inside, the sound of their steps echoing against the polished floors.

Throughout the day, Lucas took his umbrella with him, placing it in the corner of the classroom. It became a talking point among classmates, sparking stories of other rainy days and adventures. By lunchtime, Lucas and Mia had decided that they would create a "Rainy Day Club," where they would share tips on how to make the most of gloomy weather. This tiny seed of a plan blossomed into creative ideas, like art projects inspired by rain and storytelling sessions about adventures in storms.

When school finally ended, the clouds had parted ever so slightly, allowing rays of golden sunlight to break through the gray canvas. The rain had stopped, leaving glistening droplets on leaves and pavement. As Lucas and Mia stepped outside, they beamed at each other, knowing they had made the best of a rainy day.

With Stories
LEARNING ENGLISH

beamed at each other, knowing they had made the best of a rainy day. As Lucas walked home, umbrella in hand, he pondered the day's events. He realized that school was not just a place for learning from books; it was a space for forging friendships, nurturing creativity, and transforming the ordinary into the extraordinary. Whether under the shade of colorful umbrellas or sharing laughter in the rain, every experience was an opportunity to grow. That evening, as Lucas hung his umbrella by the door, he didn't just see a tool for staying dry—he saw a reminder of a day well spent, filled with laughter, friendship, and adventure. And he couldn't wait for the next rainy morning, knowing that each drop of rain was just another chance for discovery.

As Lucas walked home, the rain still gently pattering against his umbrella, a wide smile spread across his face. He thought back to the hours spent at school, where he and his friends had eagerly awaited the first droplets of rain. It was a day that had started off like any other, but as the clouds gathered and the skies turned gray, a sense of excitement filled the air.

Lucas remembered how they had all gathered by the window, pointing excitedly as the rain began to fall heavier, transforming the mundane school day into something magical. Laughter erupted as they donned their bright, colorful umbrellas and ventured outside during recess. The world had changed under the canvas of raindrops, and everything felt fresh and alive.

Each friend occupied a unique role in their little group. There was Mia, ever the jokester, who had everyone in stitches with her silly impressions and playful banter. Sam was the adventurous spirit, always daring them to jump in puddles, to race each other to the nearest tree for shelter, turning every moment into an exhilarating escapade. Lucas, who usually took the reins as the more reserved member of the group, felt empowered by the collective energy and enthusiasm of his friends.

With Stories

LEARNING ENGLISH

As they splashed through puddles, the rain seemed to weave a tapestry of memories—shared stories, spontaneous games, and, of course, the simple joys of being together. It became clear to Lucas that school was not merely a building filled with classrooms and textbooks. Instead, it was a vibrant hub where creativity flourished and friendships blossomed, where laughter could be heard echoing even on the rainiest of days.

With each step he took on his way home, he reflected on how they had transformed a dreary day into an unforgettable adventure. The joy of camaraderie mixed with the thrill of the rain had illuminated what could have been a bland routine. Lucas understood now that every moment spent with friends added layers to his experiences and enriched his life in ways that a textbook never could.

Once he arrived home, Lucas carefully placed his umbrella by the door, a sentinel that had shielded him from the downpour. But for him, it was more than just a practical tool; it was a symbol of the unforgettable day they had all shared. It reminded him not only of the rain-soaked fun he had, but also of the laughter they had exchanged, the friendships they had nurtured, and the adventures that lay just around the corner.

As the evening settled in and the clouds cleared, leaving behind the sweet scent of wet earth, Lucas gazed out the window, already looking forward to the next rainy morning. He knew it would bring with it the promise of new adventures, more laughter to share, and countless opportunities for discovery, just waiting to be embraced beneath the safety of their beloved umbrellas.

A story of resilience and wisdom

With Stories

LEARNING ENGLISH

A Story of Resilience and Wisdom

In a quaint village nestled between rolling green hills and meandering streams, there lived an old farmer named Joe. His weathered hands and silver hair told tales of a lifetime spent nurturing the land, sowing seeds, and harvesting the bounty of nature. Farmer Joe was known not just for his robust crops but for the wisdom he imparted to the young and old alike in the village.

For many decades, Joe had worked the same patch of land, a modest farm that had been passed down through generations. The quaint wooden farmhouse, with its peeling paint and sagging roof, was a testament to the years gone by. Surrounding the house were fields of corn, tomatoes, and colorful flowers that danced in the summer breeze. Each corner of the farm held memories—both joyful and sorrowful—of life's cyclical nature.

As seasons changed, so did the fortunes of Farmer Joe. In his early years, the soil was fertile, yielding abundant harvests. He would wake at dawn, listening to the chirping birds and the gentle rustle of leaves, ready to toil in the fields. Neighbors would often see him laughing with his trusty old dog, Daisy, as they worked side by side, planting and watering, a rhythmic dance of life and labor.

However, as the years progressed, times became tougher for the old farmer. Climate changes disrupted the seasons, and unseasonable storms threatened to wash away his hard work. One summer, a severe drought withered his crops, leaving the fields parched and barren. Despite the hardship, Farmer Joe never lost hope. Instead, he worked harder, investing his time in learning about modern farming techniques, seeking advice from younger farmers, and adapting to the changing environment. His resilience inspired those around him, for he believed that every challenge brought with it an opportunity to learn and grow.

But it wasn't just his farming prowess that set Farmer Joe apart; it was his profound wisdom. He would often gather the village children under the great oak tree next to his farm. With a twinkle in his eye, he would tell them stories of the past—of how the seasons teach us patience and how hard work leads to rewards. "Just like the seeds we plant," he would say, "life sometimes requires us to dig deep and nurture what we hope will grow."

With Stories
LEARNING ENGLISH

One rainy afternoon, as thunder rumbled in the distance, a young boy named Timmy sought shelter in Farmer Joe's barn. As they sat amidst the sweet scent of hay and fresh earth, Timmy spoke of his fears and dreams. He wanted to be a pilot but the thought of leaving the village and pursuing a big-city life overwhelmed him. Farmer Joe listened intently, then shared a story of his own. In his youth, he had also dreamed of traveling the world and seeing far-off places. However, it was his love for the land and community that anchored him.

"Remember, Timmy," Joe said, "wherever your journey takes you, your roots will always call you back. Sometimes the most incredible adventures are found in our own backyards."

As the years rolled on, Farmer Joe's hair turned whiter, and his steps grew slower but his spirit remained unyielded. When the villagers faced hardships, whether it was a fire, illness, or loss, Joe was always the first to lend a hand. He would often say, "We endure the storm together, and the sun will shine again." His unwavering support forged bonds that turned the village into a family.

In his twilight years, Farmer Joe became a symbol of the village's heart and soul. People from nearby towns came to listen to his stories, to learn from the wisdom of a man who had witnessed the best and worst of life. His annual harvest festival became a cherished tradition, celebrating not just the produce but the community that had flourished under his guidance.

One crisp autumn evening, as the sun dipped below the horizon, casting a warm golden glow across the fields, Farmer Joe sat outside his farmhouse, sharing stories with the villagers. As they laughed and reminisced, he felt a profound sense of gratitude. He had cultivated not just crops, but a spirit of resilience, connection, and love.

When he passed away peacefully one winter night, the village mourned the loss of their beloved farmer. But in the days that followed, they honored his legacy by planting a garden in his memory—one that would forever bring the community together, reminding them of the old farmer who had taught them the true value of hope, hard work, and the beauty of the life they had built together.

Farmer Joe may have left this world, but his spirit lived on in the hearts of those who knew him, a guiding light in times of darkness, a reminder that every seed planted carries the potential for growth, change, and community.

With Stories
LEARNING ENGLISH

When he passed away peacefully one winter night, the village mourned the profound loss of their beloved farmer, Farmer Joe, a figure whose laughter and wisdom had woven a tapestry of warmth and kindness throughout their lives. The news of his passing resonated deeply, leaving a palpable void in the hearts of villagers who had come to rely on his gentle guidance and unwavering support. For many, he was not just a farmer; he was a mentor, a friend, and a pillar of the community. As the cold winds swept through the village, carrying the whispers of sorrow, the townsfolk gathered to share stories, reminiscing about the countless harvests they celebrated together and the lessons learned under his patient care. In the days that followed, the grief they felt transformed into a collective resolve to ensure that his legacy would not fade away with the passing of time. United in their memories, the villagers decided to honor Farmer Joe by planting a garden in his memory, a living tribute to a life well-lived and a testament to the bonds he had nurtured among them. They envisioned a space brimming with vibrant flowers and lush vegetables, a place where families could come together, cultivate their shared dreams, and celebrate the changing seasons. With each shovel of earth turned and every seed sown, they felt his presence amongst them, guiding their hands and kindling their spirits.

As they worked side by side, the garden became more than just a patch of land; it evolved into a sanctuary of remembrance, a place where laughter mingled with tears, and where the cycle of life continued to flourish. Each bloom that burst forth and every ripe vegetable that ripened in the sun served as a vibrant reminder of the old farmer who had instilled in them the true value of hope, hard work, and community. It was here in this garden that they would gather to celebrate the seasons, exchange recipes, and share stories of Farmer Joe, ensuring that his lessons were passed down to the younger generations.

Though Farmer Joe may have left this world, his spirit lived on in the hearts of those who knew him, acting as a guiding light in times of darkness and uncertainty. The garden became a symbol of resilience, a reminder that every seed planted, no matter how small, carries the potential for growth, change, and unity. It demonstrated that, like the farm he tended with such love, the community could cultivate a future filled with hope. In moments of hardship, they remembered his unwavering belief in the goodness of people and the power of coming together, reinforcing their commitment to each other and their shared values.

With Stories

LEARNING ENGLISH

Thus, through the vibrant flowers and flourishing vegetables of the community garden, Farmer Joe's legacy continued to bloom, a testament to a life devoted to nurturing not just the land, but the very essence of community itself. And in the heart of the village, he would forever remain—an eternal gardener of hope, love, and togetherness.

A young couple's Parisian adventure

With Stories

LEARNING ENGLISH

A Young Couple's Parisian Adventure

Paris, the City of Lights, has long been celebrated as a romantic destination for couples. For many, it represents a dream — a place where love blossoms against the backdrop of stunning architecture, charming streets, and delectable cuisine. For two young lovers, Emma and Lucas, a trip to Paris was not just a getaway; it was a journey into the heart of their relationship, filled with adventure, discovery, and, of course, love.

Arriving in the City of Love

As their plane touched down at Charles de Gaulle Airport, excitement bubbled within them. They couldn't believe they were finally in Paris, a city they had both dreamed of visiting since childhood. Their itinerary was packed with must-see landmarks, but the couple made a pact to let spontaneity guide their exploration. After all, the most memorable experiences often happened unexpectedly.

Their first stop was the iconic Eiffel Tower. Standing beneath the towering iron lattice structure, they gazed up in awe, taking in the intricate details and sheer scale of the monument. Lucas, ever the romantic, pulled out a Polaroid camera and snapped a picture of Emma against the tower. The moment was perfect: Emma's laughter echoed as she posed, her hair catching the gentle Parisian breeze. It was a snapshot of happiness that would remind them of this magical trip for years to come.

Wandering the Streets of Montmartre

Next, they meandered through the bohemian streets of Montmartre, where the charm of cobblestone alleyways, vibrant cafés, and artistic heritage enveloped them. They stumbled upon a local art fair where painters showcased their work.

Emma, an aspiring artist, was particularly enchanted. They spent a leisurely afternoon enjoying croissants and espresso, while Emma sketched the stunning views of Sacré-Cœur Basilica from various angles. Lucas encouraged her creativity, always supportive of her passion for art.

As the sun began to set, they climbed up to the basilica's steps to watch the sky transform into a canvas of pinks and oranges. Wrapped in each other's arms, they whispered sweet nothings, feeling the world fade away around them. At that moment, they understood that the beauty of Paris was not just in its sights, but in the memories they created together.

With Stories

LEARNING ENGLISH

A Culinary Adventure
No trip to Paris would be complete without indulging in its renowned cuisine. They ventured into the heart of Le Marais, a vibrant neighborhood known for its trendy bistros and charming boutiques. Emma and Lucas decided to take a cooking class together, where they learned to prepare classic French dishes, including coq au vin and crème brûlée. The laughter and playful banter in the kitchen brought them even closer. They savored the fruits of their labor over a candlelit dinner, thrilled by the delicious flavors and the sheer joy of sharing the experience.

Romantic Evenings by the Seine
As night fell, the Seine River glimmered with reflections of the city lights. Emma and Lucas took a stroll along the water's edge, strolling hand-in-hand past historic bridges and centuries-old buildings. They stopped to listen to street musicians, their melodies adding to the romantic atmosphere. A small boat floated by, offering evening cruises, and they jumped at the chance to embark on a river adventure. Under the stars, the couple shared their dreams for the future, aspirations, and the little things that made them happy. The soft lapping of the water against the boat and the sparkling lights of the city became the backdrop to their sweet promises — to travel more, to love deeply, and to always cherish each other.

A Journey of Growth
As their trip drew to a close, Emma and Lucas reflected on the memories they had created. Paris had opened their hearts not only to each other but also to the beauty of the world around them. They learned that travel is not just about the sights seen but the experiences shared. Each moment in the City of Lights had taught them more about trust, communication, and the joys of companionship.
As they boarded their flight back home, hearts full and spirits high, they promised to hold onto the magic of Paris. They knew that their love story was just beginning and that this adventure would forever remain a cherished chapter — a reminder of the enchanting days spent in the city where love reigns supreme.

With Stories
LEARNING ENGLISH

As the sun began to set on their last evening in Paris, Emma and Lucas found themselves perched on a quaint café terrace overlooking the Seine River. With glasses of velvety red wine in hand and the sweet sounds of a nearby accordion playing a nostalgic tune, they reflected on the moments that had defined their trip. Each sip brought back vivid memories—strolling hand-in-hand through the cobblestone streets of Montmartre, marveling at the artistry in the Louvre, and sharing laughter over croissants at a bustling boulangerie. Paris had truly unveiled not just its iconic landmarks but had also entwined their hearts deeper together in the tapestry of life.

The journey they had embarked upon was not merely about visiting a new city; it was a transformative experience that reshaped their understanding of connection. Together, they discovered that travel serves as a mirror, reflecting not only the beauty of the external world but also the inner landscape of their relationship. They learned that the true essence of travel lies in the shared moments—the quiet strolls under the Eiffel Tower at twilight, the heated debates about art as they stood in front of a Monet, and the spontaneous adventures that led them down hidden alleyways. Each experience carved new facets of trust and communication, allowing their bond to flourish amid the vibrant energy of the City of Lights.

As they boarded their flight back home, filled with the aroma of freshly baked baguettes and the laughter of the streets still echoing in their minds, they exchanged knowing glances, their hearts brimming with gratitude for the journey they had crafted together. They relished the thought that this was not an ending but a beautiful beginning; the spark of their love ignited further by every magical moment spent in a city that celebrates love in all its forms. The promise they made—to hold onto the magic of Paris—was a commitment to nurturing their relationship and embracing the adventures that lay ahead.

They knew that this trip would forever be a cherished chapter in their love story, a vibrant reminder of the enchanting days spent in a city where time seemed to stand still, and love was palpable in every corner. As they flew above the clouds, their hearts soared with the possibilities of tomorrow, knowing full well that while they may have left Paris, the lessons learned and memories made would remain a part of them, forever guiding their journey of growth together. Each trip they took beyond this would be a new canvas, an opportunity to paint the landscape of their lives with the colors of experience, trust, and love.

With Stories

LEARNING ENGLISH

A Story of Resilience and Hope
Introduction

In the bustling world of literature, there are countless stories waiting to be told, yet some tales remain tucked away in the shadows, yearning for a voice. One such story is that of a young girl named Aisha, who, despite the hardships of poverty, embodies resilience, dreams, and an indomitable spirit. As a writer, John takes it upon himself to weave Aisha's narrative into the fabric of society's consciousness, shedding light on the struggles of the underprivileged while celebrating their strength.

Aisha's World

Aisha lives in a small, dilapidated neighborhood on the outskirts of the city, surrounded by crumbling buildings and the constant hum of despair. The streets she walks are filled with the echoes of laughter from children who have little to smile about, playing amidst the debris of a forgotten world. The scarcity of food, proper education, and basic healthcare shapes her reality, but it does not define her. Aisha is a dreamer; she often escapes into the worlds of the books she borrows from her ragged school library.

John's journey begins as he visits Aisha's neighborhood for research, hoping to capture the authenticity of her experiences. As he walks through the narrow lanes, he witnesses not only poverty but also community, resilience, and a flicker of hope amidst the struggle. He encounters Aisha one day, sitting under a tree, her nose buried in a worn-out book. Intrigued by her determination to learn, John strikes up conversation, and what begins as a chance encounter quickly blossoms into an inspiring friendship.

The power of storytelling

With Stories

LEARNING ENGLISH

The Power of Storytelling

In crafting Aisha's narrative, John aims to amplify the voices of the marginalized, reminding his readers that their experiences, though often overlooked, are crucial to understanding the broader social context. Through Aisha, John presents a lens through which readers can see the struggles faced by countless young girls around the world. Their dreams, aspirations, and rights are often stifled by circumstances outside their control.

For John, writing Aisha's story is about more than storytelling; it's a call to action. He hopes to inspire readers to engage with social issues, advocate for change, and support initiatives that empower girls like Aisha. By bringing her story to life, he challenges stereotypes and emphasizes the importance of education, opportunity, and support.

Conclusion: Aisha's Journey Continues

As John completes his manuscript, he reflects on the profound impact that Aisha and her community have had on him. Her journey is far from over, and he knows that the story he has told is just a part of the larger narrative of resilience and hope that encompasses countless lives.

In sharing Aisha's story, John not only elevates her voice but also invites his readers to be part of her journey, to dream alongside her, and to create a world where every girl has the opportunity to shine. Ultimately, Aisha's tale serves as a reminder that within every struggle lies the potential for strength, growth, and an unwavering hope for a brighter tomorrow.

With Stories

LEARNING ENGLISH

Aisha's Journey Continues

As John finalizes the last touches on his manuscript, he pauses for a moment, allowing his thoughts to wander back to Aisha and the vibrant community that has so profoundly impacted his life. He finds himself reflecting deeply on her journey—a journey that is far from its conclusion. Each page he has written captures only a fragment of a much larger tapestry woven from the intricate threads of resilience crafted by Aisha and those around her. He understands that her story, while powerful in its singularity, is but a small piece of a grand narrative that extends into the lives of countless individuals who also embody the spirit of perseverance and hope.

In choosing to share Aisha's story with the world, John takes on the sacred responsibility of not just telling her narrative but also elevating her voice to the forefront. He recognizes that by doing so, he is inviting his readers to walk alongside her, to dream alongside her, and to envision a future where every girl, regardless of her circumstances, has the chance to realize her dreams and aspirations. He envisions readers feeling inspired to join Aisha in her quest for knowledge, empowerment, and self-discovery. The journey they embark on together fosters a collective understanding of the challenges and triumphs faced by girls everywhere, creating a bridge between their lives and the lives of those portrayed in the pages of his book.

Ultimately, Aisha's tale resonates beyond the confines of the pages; it serves as a poignant reminder that within every struggle lies the potential for transformation. Each obstacle she encounters becomes a stepping stone toward strength and growth, illuminating the path to a future brimming with possibility. John hopes to instill in his readers the belief that hope is a powerful force, one that can illuminate even the darkest of times and pave the way for a brighter tomorrow. As Aisha continues her journey, John feels a renewed sense of purpose—not just to tell her story, but to inspire action, to ignite a movement in which every girl is seen, heard, and given the chance to shine her light upon the world.

A journey of love and healing

With Stories

LEARNING ENGLISH

A Journey of Love and Healing: A Story of Compassion and Connection"

In a bustling hospital where beeps and nurses' footsteps were heard, the story of Dr. Emily Harrison unfolded: a story of compassion, resilience, and an unexpected romance that thrived amid the challenges of a patient's illness.

Dr. Harrison was known for his exceptional abilities as an oncologist. Known for his unwavering dedication to his patients, Dr. Harrison worked tirelessly, even beyond the hours recommended by his colleagues. His patients admired him not only for his medical expertise, but also for his ability to listen, comfort, and support them through their most difficult times. A patient named Sarah Mitchell would soon become an important part of Dr. Harrison's journey as both a doctor and a human being.

Sarah was always a healthy person until life took a brutal turn. At the age of 32, she was diagnosed with stage three breast cancer. The news was devastating—not just for Sarah, but also for her friends and family. He was a lively soul known for his liveliness, laughter, and love of adventure. Suddenly, his life was marred by the uncertainties of the disease.

When Sarah first met Dr. Harrison, they formed an instant bond. With his warm smile and understanding demeanor, Dr. Harrison was no ordinary doctor in a white coat; It was a glimmer of hope. Sarah often said that the way Dr. Harrison explained his treatment options was more like a conversation between friends than a clinical discussion. With each visit, Sarah felt stronger to face her illness.

Their relationship deepened as they struggled with chemotherapy and the side effects that followed. Dr. Harrison became not only a physician, but also a confidant. They shared stories about their lives; Sarah talked about her travels before she was diagnosed, her love of cooking, and her dreams of one day running a marathon again. Dr. Harrison shared snippets from his personal life: his passion for painting and his desire to make a difference in the world through medicine.

With Stories
LEARNING ENGLISH

But in the midst of this professional bond, feelings began to blur. Dr. Harrison noticed that Sarah was drawn to her stamina and joie de vivre. Despite the bleak prognosis, Sarah's soul shone brightly. The laughter they shared during the consultations often turned into a refuge from the harshness of reality. Small moments, such as suggesting bright nail polish colors to lift Sarah's spirits, made her clinic environment feel more human.

But as the weeks turned into months, the truth came out. Sarah's cancer treatment was challenging, and there were days when hope was fleeting. Every time he faced a setback, Dr. Harrison was right there by his side, balancing his role as a doctor with his deepening emotional investment. On one of those difficult evenings, as she sat on the hospital balcony overlooking a city teeming with life outside, Dr. Harrison noticed that his feelings for Sarah had turned into something deeper; a love he had never experienced before.

Navigating the ethical complexities of their relationship posed a challenge. Dr. Harrison was well aware of the professional boundaries that needed to be maintained in health care. Still, love is a powerful force. They found moments to bond on dates outside; Short talk in the hallways, evasive glances, and shared smiles that mean more than words can ever convey.

Finally, a critical moment came when Sarah's health began to deteriorate. Faced with the fragility of life, Dr. Harrison decided to confront his feelings. On a quiet evening in Sarah's hospital room, with golden sunset rays streaming in through the window, Dr. Harrison took a leap of faith. She confessed her feelings, revealing her heart as she acknowledged the complexity of their situation.

She was surprised to see that Sarah felt the same way. The bond between them transcended the patient-doctor dynamic and turned into a love story full of difficulties. They talked about the importance of proceeding carefully in relationships, as well as the possible challenges and implications. They decided not to fully pursue their romance until Sarah's treatment was complete, but hope blossomed in their hearts.

Sarah's journey wasn't over yet. With the unwavering support of Dr. Harrison, she bravely endured each day. Their bond has been a source of strength for both of them It's a reminder that love can thrive even in the toughest of circumstances.

With Stories
LEARNING ENGLISH

In conclusion, the story of Drs. Emily Harrison and Sarah Mitchell is not just about the disease; It's a reminder of how deep an impact human connection can have on the healing process. He emphasizes the importance of empathy and compassion, qualities that transform ordinary medical interactions into human experiences. Eventually, love became an important part of Sarah's healing journey; A healing power that transcends the challenges that life throws at them. And for Dr. Harrison, loving Sarah was a profound reminder of why he chose medicine; It wasn't just about healing bodies, it was about nurturing souls.

As Sarah continued her battle with cancer, Dr. Harrison remained steadfast, not only as a doctor, but also as someone's partner in hope, love, and life. Together, they would navigate the uncertain waters of illness, trying to create a future full of possibilities and strengthening their love story in the process.

With Stories

LEARNING ENGLISH

The story of Dr. Emily Harrison and Sarah Mitchell reveals the transformative power of human relationships in the healing process, changing the distribution of a single human struggle. This story reveals that health is not only limited to physical healing but also that spiritual and emotional support is at least as important as physical health. The bond between Harrison and Sarah deepens with the challenges faced by events, both are strengthened by love and devotion to each other.

Empathy and treatment are essential qualities necessary for care and healing. Harrison has a presence alongside Sarah not only as a doctor, but also as a friend, comrade, and a life partner. This relationship turns an ordinary examination into an emotional experience, eliminating people's experience of loneliness as they face the odds. Sarah's moment of facing challenges is made more meaningful by Dr. Harrison's love and support for her.

Sarah's recovery process is not just about trying to regain her physical health; At the same time, it contains a process of transformation in the depths of the human soul. Love becomes one of the most important forces in these journeys, and each day offers a new source of hope in the treatment process. This love manifests itself as a healing force in the various choices that life has to offer.

The more Harrison loves Sarah, the more he understands why medical lockdown. This industry not only repairs physical bodies but also feeds people's souls. This situation shows how the love between two people is deepened and strengthened in the treatment process while revealing the human developments of medicine.

As Sarah continues her battle with cancer, Dr. Harrison's dedication to her during this challenging time reinforces her resolve not only as a healthcare provider, but also as a person who offers emotional support. Together, the two navigate the water of eventful events, trying to shape their hopes, loving moments, and new dreams together. In the process, as the distribution of lifespan comes, the love story between them also becomes stronger. In conclusion, the story of Drs. Emily Harrison and Sarah Mitchell inspires us as an example of the courage of the power of human bonds and their role in the healing process.

With Stories
LEARNING ENGLISH

After the match was over, we shared our contact information and promised to stay in touch. As I walked away from the arena that night, I couldn't shake the excitement of meeting him. I felt as if fate had intervened and presented me with an opportunity too important to ignore.

In the weeks that followed, our conversations continued. James offered me mentorship, guided me through my career uncertainties, and helped me chart a path toward my own aspirations. With her encouragement, I began to explore new ventures, push my boundaries, and embrace the possibility of success. He helped me identify my strengths, giving me advice that was both practical and empowering.

Through this unexpected encounter in a boxing match, I learned that wealth is not just about wealth; It's also about the connections we make and the people we meet along the way. James has shown me that success is not just a destination, but a journey filled with learning, resilience, and growth.

When I think about that night, I realize how important it was. The seemingly mundane event of a boxing match became the backdrop of an extraordinary bond. I am grateful to have had the chance to meet a man whose wealth of experience and guidance has inspired me to pursue my dreams and redefine my understanding of success.

Looking ahead, I carry with me the lessons I learned both in the ring and from James; It's a reminder that sometimes the best opportunities come when we least expect it. Life, just like boxing, is about seizing the moment, taking risks, and embracing the punches that come our way.

With Stories
LEARNING ENGLISH

Through these unexpected encounters I had in a boxing match, it was possible to understand that service is not just about wealth. Wealth involves material accumulations; The relationships and friendships we build and the relationships we build with the people we know along the way are also important parts of this service. James, whom I met in that ring, showed me that success is not just a destination, but rather a journey full of resilience and personal growth and learning. Whatever happens in the distribution of life, we need to learn the lessons that this journey offers us.

When I live that night, it happens in a much better way how important the experience is. The boxing match, which was a seemingly ordinary event, actually laid the foundations for an extraordinary bond for me. Meeting James during this struggle, witnessing his experiences, and having the opportunity to pursue my dreams under his guidance was a great inspiration to me. What he followed played a big role in me reshaping my understanding of success; Because real wealth is in being able to evaluate life offers and establish strong bonds with people.

Looking ahead, I plan to carry the lessons I learned from James and what I experienced in the ring there. Because sometimes it's important to survive the best opportunities when we least expect them. Life is like their books; It is a struggle based on seizing the moment, taking risks and bravely facing all the challenges that come our way. These values, which I learned in the boxing ring, now guide me in my daily life. All these experiences, impressions limited to only one sport, remain fundamentals, valid in all areas of life.

With Stories
LEARNING ENGLISH

Looking ahead, I think about how important my experiences in the ring and the lessons I learned from James have been in my life. I plan to apply these experiences not only in the boxing ring, but also in my daily life. Because I have observed that the best opportunities that life brings often come at the most unexpected moments. This shows how critical it is to survive and succeed.

Life is just like those books at our bedside; Every page offers a new adventure, a new lesson, and a new opportunity. Seizing the moment, taking risks, and boldly facing the challenges that come our way are essential to moving forward in life. The experiences I have gained in the boxing ring and the values I have learned are now guiding me. Every punch, every single match, has become not only a physical challenge, but also a lesson in my mental and emotional resilience.

All these experiences have a special meaning for me and remain valid not only in a limited sport such as boxing, but in all areas of life. Because every fight in the ring shapes the character of the individual and makes the person stronger. Being able to stand tall in the face of life's challenges is actually a situation that reflects my struggles in the boxing ring in a similar way. Be that as it may, the lessons I learned from these experiences will remain the cornerstones for me. As a result, the lessons I've learned, both in boxing and in life, are constantly putting me on the path to becoming a better individual.

With Stories
LEARNING ENGLISH

How a Gamer Won a Basketball and Transformed His Game

In an unexpected turn of events that illustrates the unpredictable nature of gaming culture, an avid gamer has recently made headlines after winning an official basketball during a competitive gaming event. This incident has not only sparked conversations across various platforms about the intersection of traditional sports and esports but also inspired a narrative about the versatility of players in adapting their skills from virtual realms to the physical world.

The Event

The recent gaming tournament, held in a packed auditorium, attracted numerous competitors and fans, all eager to showcase their skills in various popular titles. Among the many activities stacked into the event was a surprise segment: a mini basketball competition designed to promote physical activity among gamers. Participants could win prizes that ranged from gaming gear to merchandise, with the grand prize being a signed basketball from a well-known professional player.

The Gamer

Meet Jordan "Jjazz" Smith, a 22-year-old streamer and avid gamer known for his prowess in games like "Call of Duty" and "FIFA". Jjazz is emblematic of a growing community of gamers who seamlessly commit to nurturing their passions within and outside their screens. While not previously known for his athletic abilities, Jjazz decided to participate in the basketball challenge on a whim, driven by a desire to engage with fellow gamers and add a bit of physical activity to his day.

With Stories
LEARNING ENGLISH

The Winning Moment

With his gamer instincts sharp and adrenaline at an all-time high, Jjazz managed to sink several impressive shots against his opponents, including a buzzer-beater that not only sealed his victory but also had the crowd erupting in cheers. His charisma and infectious energy won over the audience, who suddenly saw him in a new light—not just as a gamer, but as an athlete in his own right.

The Aftermath

Winning the basketball was a pivotal moment for Jjazz, inspiring him to take a closer look at his physical fitness. He began incorporating basketball drills and fitness routines into his daily life, finding it an enjoyable way to balance his intense gaming sessions with much-needed exercise. "Winning that ball was just the push I needed," he reflected in a post-tournament interview. "It reminded me that being a gamer doesn't mean I can't achieve other physical feats."

Community Response

The response from the gaming community has been overwhelmingly positive. Jjazz's journey resonated with many, leading to a wave of support from fellow gamers who also started sharing their athletic endeavors. Social media platforms filled with hashtag challenges like #GamerToAthlete, encouraging others to step out from behind their screens and participate in physical activities they enjoy. Moreover, gaming brands took notice, realizing the potential benefits of promoting fitness collaborations with professionals in traditional sports. Many companies are now looking into sponsorships and programs that celebrate the holistic lifestyles of gamers who want to push boundaries in both digital and physical arenas.

Conclusion

Jjazz's story underlines a larger narrative: the evolving identity of gamers who refuse to be pigeonholed into a singular role. By winning a basketball and embracing the joys of sport, he has drawn attention to the possibilities that lie at the intersection of gaming and traditional athletics. As more gamers recognize their potential and engage with

With Stories
LEARNING ENGLISH

the physical world, it's clear that the landscape of both communities is changing—for the better.

In a world increasingly dominated by screens, Jjazz reminds us that sometimes, stepping outside is one of the best moves you can make. Whether you're holding a controller or a basketball, the spirit of competition and community remains the same.

With Stories
LEARNING ENGLISH

Jjazz's journey not only highlights his personal achievements, but it also underscores a much larger narrative about the evolving identity of gamers in today's society. There once was a time when gamers were often pigeonholed into a singular role, associated with a particular set of behaviors or interests. However, Jjazz serves as a powerful example of how the gaming community is breaking free from these outdated stereotypes. By triumphantly winning a basketball game and enthusiastically embracing the joys of traditional sports, he has illuminated the exciting possibilities that emerge at the crossroads of gaming and athletics.

As more gamers like Jjazz begin to explore their full potential and actively engage with the physical world around them, it becomes increasingly evident that the landscapes of both gaming and sports communities are experiencing a significant transformation—for the better. This evolution signifies not just a merging of interests, but a broader, more inclusive understanding of what it means to be a gamer in the modern age. No longer confined to the virtual realms of their favorite video games, these individuals are integrating real-world experiences into their identities, allowing for a richer, more diverse exploration of their passions.

In an era where screens often dominate our daily lives, Jjazz's story serves as a poignant reminder that sometimes the best decision you can make is simply to step outside. Whether you find yourself gripping a gaming controller or shooting hoops with a basketball, the fundamental spirit of competition, camaraderie, and community remains constant. It emphasizes that the thrill of competition transcends the boundaries of digital and physical play, fostering connections among individuals who share a love for both gaming and sports. This evolving narrative encourages all of us to embrace the hybrid identity that lies within, inspiring future generations of gamers to explore their potential beyond the pixels and discover the joys of movement, teamwork, and genuine human interaction.

With Stories
LEARNING ENGLISH

A Chance Encounter

Officer Jake Thompson was having a busy day patrolling the streets of his small town when he received a call about a minor traffic accident on Maple Street. As he arrived at the scene, he quickly assessed the situation. Two cars had collided, but fortunately, no one appeared to be seriously injured.

As he approached the vehicles, he noticed a young woman standing next to one of the cars, looking a bit shaken but otherwise fine. Her name was Emily, and she had a warm smile that somehow put him at ease despite the chaos around them.

"Are you okay?" Jake asked, his voice calm and reassuring.

"Yeah, just a bit rattled," Emily replied, tucking a strand of hair behind her ear. "This is not how I imagined my day would go."

Jake chuckled softly, "I think that's something we can both agree on. Let's get your information sorted out."

As they exchanged details, they found themselves lost in conversation. Emily was a local artist, and they connected over their love for the town and its hidden gems. Jake felt an unexpected spark between them, a connection that made the stressful day worth it.

After ensuring that both parties were safe and that the accident report would be filed, Jake hesitated for a moment. "If you'd like, maybe I could show you around town sometime? I know a great little café that serves the best coffee."

Emily's eyes lit up. "I'd like that. Maybe I can even show you some of my favorite spots too."

As they parted ways, Jake felt a blend of excitement and hope. What began as a routine day of duty had unexpectedly turned into a potential new chapter in his life.

Over the next few weeks, their casual meetings turned into regular dates. They explored art galleries, shared stories over coffee, and built a connection that was both effortless and genuine.

With Stories
LEARNING ENGLISH

Jake found himself falling for Emily, and as their relationship blossomed, he realized that sometimes the most beautiful moments arise from the most unexpected circumstances.

Over the next few weeks, what began as casual meetings gradually evolved into regular dates that filled their evenings with joy and laughter. They discovered charming art galleries tucked away in corners of the city, where they marveled at vibrant canvases and intricate sculptures, each piece sparking lively discussions that deepened their understanding of one another. Between the strokes of paint and the flickers of inspiration, they shared stories over steaming cups of coffee, recounting tales from their pasts, dreams for the future, and everything in between. Each conversation seemed to weave them closer together, building a connection that felt both effortless and genuine, as if they were two pieces of a puzzle that had finally found their match.

As days turned into weeks, Jake found himself increasingly captivated by Emily's warmth and humor. Her laughter was like music to his ears, and the way her eyes sparkled when she spoke about her passions made his heart race. With every shared experience, whether it was a simple walk in the park or a late-night chat under the stars, he realized he was falling for her in a way he had never anticipated. The relationship was blossoming beautifully, marked by tender moments and shared glances that spoke volumes.

Amidst the growing affection, he had a profound revelation: sometimes, the most beautiful moments in life arise from the most unexpected circumstances. What had started as a simple acquaintance had transformed into a meaningful partnership that challenged his perceptions of love and connection. As he reflected on their time together, he couldn't help but feel grateful for the serendipity that had brought them together, making him eager to see where this thrilling journey would lead. It was a reminder that love often blooms in the unlikeliest of places, and for Jake and Emily, this was just the beginning of their story.

With Stories
LEARNING ENGLISH

A Day of Adventure: Alisa's Trip to the Zoo

It was a bright and sunny Saturday morning when Alisa woke up with a sense of excitement fluttering in her chest. Today was the day she had been eagerly anticipating for weeks—her trip to the zoo! After having carefully planned the outing with her family, Alisa could hardly wait to step into the wonderful world of wildlife.

With her favorite blue dress and a pair of comfortable sneakers, Alisa rushed through breakfast, her eyes sparkling with delight. Her parents, equally enthusiastic, gathered snacks and a camera to capture the day's memories. With everything packed and ready, they hopped into the car, and soon they were on their way, with laughter and music filling the air.

As they arrived at the zoo, Alisa's eyes widened with wonder. The entrance was adorned with vibrant murals of animals, and she could hear the distant sounds of chirping birds and roaring lions. With a bounce in her step, she led the way through the gates, her heart racing in anticipation of the adventures that lay ahead.

Their first stop was the majestic elephant enclosure. Alisa was in awe as she watched these gentle giants splash water on themselves with their trunks. She learned from the zookeeper that elephants communicate through vocalizations and ear movements, a fact that intrigued her. She giggled as one of the elephants playfully sprayed water in her direction, and she felt the cool mist on her face.

From there, the family moved on to the giraffe exhibit. Alisa was thrilled to see the long-necked creatures munching on leaves high above. She looked up at the tallest giraffe and exclaimed, "I wish I could reach that high!" Her parents chuckled and snapped photos as Alisa stood on her tiptoes, trying to measure herself against her new favorite animals.

With Stories
LEARNING ENGLISH

Next, they wandered to the exotic bird section, where colorful parrots and singing canaries flitted around. Alisa was fascinated by the vibrant plumage of the birds and stood mesmerized as one of the parrots danced and mimicked sounds. She couldn't help but clap her hands in joy. "I wish I could take one home!" she said, her imagination running wild.

After a morning full of marveling at the animals, it was time for a lunch break. They found a cozy picnic spot near the children's zoo, where Alisa enjoyed her favorite sandwiches while watching kids pet goats and rabbits. The cheerful atmosphere was infectious, and Alisa couldn't resist joining in on the fun. She spent a delightful hour feeding the animals, her laughter mingling with their bleats and squeaks.

Refreshed, Alisa and her family headed towards the big cat exhibit. Standing before the glass enclosure, Alisa's eyes sparkled as she watched a magnificent lion basking in the sun. "He's so strong and beautiful!" she whispered in awe. Her parents explained how lions live in prides and shared stories of their majestic prowess in the wild. Alisa was completely captivated.

As the afternoon waned, they ventured towards the aquarium section. The dark, cool environment was a refreshing contrast to the sunny day outside. Alisa's eyes widened as she gazed at the vibrant fish, graceful jellyfish, and even a playful sea otter. The otter made faces at the crowd, and Alisa laughed heartily, completely enchanted by its antics.

With the day drawing to a close, Alisa and her family made one last stop—a gift shop filled with delightful souvenirs. Alisa carefully chose a plush giraffe to remind her of the incredible day she had spent exploring the wonders of the zoo.

With Stories
LEARNING ENGLISH

As they left the zoo, Alisa felt a sense of happiness swelling in her heart. She had seen so many incredible animals, learned about their habitats, and made wonderful memories with her family. The sun began to set, painting the sky in hues of orange and pink, as they headed home.

Later that night, as Alisa snuggled in bed with her new giraffe, she realized that today wasn't just about seeing animals; it was about feeling connected to nature and the thrill of discovery. With dreams of elephants, giraffes, and playful otters dancing in her head, Alisa drifted off to sleep, already looking forward to her next adventure.

As they left the zoo, Alisa felt a delightful sense of happiness swelling in her heart, wrapping around her like a warm blanket. The day had been filled with joy and wonder, as she had marveled at the majestic lions lounging in the sun, watched the playful antics of monkeys swinging through their habitat, and gasped in awe at the graceful movements of the towering giraffes. Each exhibit had unveiled a new world, and Alisa soaked in the knowledge shared by the friendly zookeepers about the animals' behaviors, diets, and the unique ecosystems they thrived in.

With her family by her side, every moment seemed more precious. They shared laughter as they pointed out the funny faces the capybaras made and gasped together as they observed the sleek dolphins leaping through the air during their entertaining show. Together, they captured the day's magic in photographs, preserving memories that would surely bring smiles for years to come. As they strolled through the zoo, each corner they turned revealed another exciting creature and another fascinating story, forging a deeper bond between Alisa and her loved ones with each shared experience.

With Stories
LEARNING ENGLISH

As the sun began to set, its golden rays filtered through the trees, casting long shadows on the pathway and painting the sky in breathtaking hues of orange and pink. The tranquil beauty of the evening brought a sense of closure to an unforgettable day as they made their way home, still buzzing with excitement. The gentle warmth of the fading sun kissed Alisa's cheeks, and she felt a surge of gratitude for the time spent together as a family.

Later that night, as Alisa snuggled under her cozy blankets, clutching her new plush giraffe tightly, she reflected on the day's adventures. She realized that today wasn't just about the thrill of seeing animals in their enclosures; it was about the profound connection she felt with nature and the exhilaration of discovery that filled her spirit. Each moment spent observing the creatures and learning about their lives deepened her appreciation for the natural world around her.

With vivid images of elephants trumpeting, giraffes stretching their long necks to nibble leaves from tall trees, and playful otters sliding down rocks splashing joyously in her head, Alisa began to drift off to sleep. She felt a sense of peace envelop her, eager to dream of the wild and wonderful creatures she had encountered. Her heart was already filled with excitement as she looked forward to her next adventure, wondering what new experiences and discoveries awaited her in the great, beautiful world beyond her window.

Later that night, as Alisa snuggled under her cozy blankets, wrapping herself in their warmth like a soft hug, she clutched her new plush giraffe tightly to her chest. Its fabric was soft and comforting, a reminder of the delightful day she had experienced. As she lay there in the soft glow of her bedside lamp, her mind wandered back to the day's adventures, replaying the memories like a cherished film.

She realized that today wasn't just about the thrilling spectacle of seeing animals in their enclosures—-it was about so much more. It was about the profound connection she felt with nature, an invisible thread that linked her heart to the wild world outside her window. With each glance at the magnificent creatures, she found herself captivated, reveling in the exhilaration of discovery that filled her spirit like a rushing river. Each encounter was a revelation, unveiling new layers of understanding and appreciation for the intricate lives of the beings that shared the planet with her.

With Stories
LEARNING ENGLISH

As she reminisced, vivid images danced in her mind—elephants trumpeting in the distance, their majestic bodies moving gracefully across the savanna, the sound echoing like a powerful anthem of nature. She could picture giraffes, those towering beauties, stretching their long necks to nibble leaves from the treetops, their gentle eyes filled with a peaceful wisdom. Then, there were the playful otters, darting about with boundless energy, sliding down the smooth rocks and splashing joyously into the cool water, their laughter resonating in a wild, carefree symphony.

With these vibrant scenes swirling in her head, Alisa began to drift softly into slumber, her thoughts slowly fading into a dreamy haze. She felt a sense of peace envelop her, like a warm blanket on a chilly night, wrapping her in comfort as she surrendered to sleep. In her heart, an anticipation bubbled up, eager to dream of the wild and wonderful creatures she had encountered, to relive their antics and enjoy their company in the realm of her imagination.

As her eyelids grew heavy, her heart filled with excitement for the adventures yet to come. She eagerly looked forward to her next adventure, wondering what new experiences and discoveries awaited her in the great, beautiful world beyond her window. What other magical animals would she meet? What secrets of the wilderness would she uncover? The possibilities danced in her mind, keeping her afloat in a sea of dreams filled with wonder as she finally surrendered to the sweet embrace of sleep.

As her eyelids grew heavy, gently fluttering like the delicate wings of a butterfly, her heart swelled with an exhilarating anticipation for the countless adventures that lay just beyond the horizon. Each thump of her heart echoed the thrill of unknown journeys, whispering to her soul that excitement was on the cusp, waiting to be unearthed. She eagerly looked forward to her next escapade, her mind racing with questions and curiosity about what new experiences and dazzling discoveries awaited her in the great, beautiful world that spread out like a colorful tapestry beyond her window.

With Stories
LEARNING ENGLISH

She envisioned herself wandering through lush forests, where sunlight filtered through the canopy, casting playful shadows on the ground. What other magical animals would she meet? Perhaps a wise old owl with stories etched in its ancient eyes or a mischievous fox that danced through the underbrush, both curious and clever. Would she encounter gentle deer grazing peacefully, their coats glistening like polished amber in the dappled light? Each creature she imagined sparkled with personality, promising companionship and wisdom in their own unique language.

Thoughts of the wilderness filled her with wonder. What secrets of the natural world would she uncover? Maybe she would stumble upon a hidden waterfall, its water sparkling like diamonds as it cascaded into a crystal-clear pool below. Or perhaps she'd follow a narrow, winding path that led her to an uncharted cave, its walls adorned with ancient drawings that told the tales of people long gone. Every possibility danced in her mind, swirling and twirling like leaves caught in a gentle autumn breeze, keeping her afloat in a sea of dreams brimming with enchantment and excitement.

As the comforting weight of sleep began to envelop her, she surrendered herself to the sweet embrace of slumber, allowing the vibrant images to swirl around her like a gentle whirlpool. With the promise of adventure lingering in the corners of her mind, she drifted off, her heart racing with joy at the thought of the magical journeys that awaited her. Each breath brought her closer to her dreams, and with every sigh, she let go of the day, ready to leap into the extraordinary realms of her imagination, where anything was possible and the world was alive with wonder.

With Stories
LEARNING ENGLISH

A Heartwarming Cake-Baking Adventure

Introduction

Baking a cake is often an act of love, especially when it's shared between a mother and daughter. This sweet recipe for bonding combines flour, sugar, and a sprinkle of laughter, creating not just a delicious dessert but also cherished memories. Join us as we explore a beautiful story where a simple kitchen endeavor blossoms into a day filled with creativity, connection, and life lessons.

Setting the Scene

On a sunny Saturday morning, the kitchen was alive with the sounds of the world outside: birds chirping, a gentle breeze rustling the trees, and the faint hum of traffic in the distance. Inside their cozy home, Sarah, a spirited seven-year-old with a wild mane of curls, hurriedly descended the stairs. Her excitement was palpable as she burst into the kitchen, where her mom, Emily, was preparing for the day's special activity—baking a cake.

"What kind of cake are we making today, Mom?" Sarah asked, her eyes sparkling with anticipation.

"We're going to make your favorite—chocolate cake!" Emily replied, smiling. Little did they know that this day would be about more than just baking; it would be a day of laughter, learning, and love.

The Baking Begins

With ingredients spread out on the countertop, Emily explained the steps to making the cake. "First, we need to gather everything we need," she said. Sarah eagerly measured out sugar, flour, and cocoa powder, her tiny hands working hard to keep up with her mom's organized rhythm.

As they mixed the dry ingredients, Emily shared a bit of what she knew about baking. "Did you know that baking is like a science experiment? Each ingredient plays an important role!" Sarah listened intently, her curiosity piqued. The bond of learning now flourished between them as they whipped eggs and melted butter. Sarah's giggles filled the kitchen as she accidentally flicked a bit of flour on her mother's nose during the mixing process.

With Stories
LEARNING ENGLISH

"Oops! Now you look like a cupcake!" Sarah laughed.
Emily wiped the flour off her face and grinned, "Just adding some extra sweetness to the day!"

Creativity Takes Center Stage

With the batter mixed to perfection, it was time to pour it into the pans. Emily handed Sarah a spatula, and as they did this together, they began discussing what to do once the cake was baked. "Should we add sprinkles or maybe some fruit on top?" Emily asked.
"Can we make it a rainbow?" Sarah suggested excitedly, her imagination painting vivid pictures in her mind.
"Well, why not? We can make a rainbow of frosting with all the colors we have!" Emily replied, thrilled at her daughter's creativity.
With the cake in the oven, they turned their attention to preparing the colorful frosting. They carefully mixed batches of icing, adding food coloring with meticulous precision. Each tube of color brought out laughter and playful experimentation. They painted their own versions of a rainbow on paper towels, turning the process into an artistic project that brought them even closer.

The Scent of Success

As the aroma of baking chocolate filled the home, Emily and Sarah couldn't resist peeking into the oven, their hearts racing with anticipation. "It's rising beautifully, just like I knew it would!" Emily exclaimed, pride swelling as she looked at her daughter.
While they waited for the cake to cool, they shared stories and giggles. Emily told Sarah about her own childhood baking experiences, how she learned from her mother, and how she cherished those memories. They talked about the importance of patience and precision in baking, and how each moment spent in the kitchen was a chance to create something wonderful together.

With Stories
LEARNING ENGLISH

The Grand Finale

Once the cakes had cooled, it was time to frost. Emily guided Sarah as they layered the cakes and spread the frosting on top. With each stroke of the spatula, Sarah's eyes sparkled with delight at the vibrant colors and their whimsical creations.

When they finished, the cake was a beautiful masterpiece fit for a party, with bright layers and colorful frosting artfully swirling around it. Proud of their work, they took a moment to admire their creation before slicing into it.

As they each took a bite, a moment of silence fell over them, followed by an explosion of laughter. "It's perfect!" Sarah exclaimed, chocolate frosting smudging her cheek.

"It's not just the cake that's perfect; it's our day together," Emily replied, hugging her daughter close. "This was more than just baking; it was about creating memories."

Once the cakes had cooled to a delightful room temperature, it was finally time to begin the frosting process. Emily, full of enthusiasm and expertise, took the lead as she guided Sarah through the steps. They carefully layered the moist cakes, each one a perfect circle of golden perfection, as they prepared to decorate. With their assortment of brightly colored frostings sprawled out before them—vivid pinks, electric blues, sunny yellows, and rich chocolate—the excitement in the kitchen was palpable. Sarah's eyes sparkled with delight as she witnessed the beautiful array of colors, and her imagination ignited at the thought of the whimsical creations that they would bring to life.

With each stroke of the spatula, Sarah unleashed her creativity, spreading the frosting with joyful abandon. She marveled at how the colors blended and contrasted, forming artistic swirls and patterns across the surface of the cake. The once-simple layers transformed before their eyes into a vibrant masterpiece that radiated fun and festivity, perfectly suited for a lively party celebration. As the last dollop of frosting was smoothed out, they paused for a moment, stepping back to admire their handiwork. The cake stood tall and proud, adorned with bright layers and colorful frosting artfully swirling around it like a whimsical rainbow.

With Stories
LEARNING ENGLISH

Filled with a sweet sense of accomplishment, the two of them exchanged satisfied smiles, entirely captivated by their creation. It was not just a cake; it was a symbol of their teamwork, joy, and shared laughter. After capturing a few pictures to commemorate their baking adventure, Emily reached for a serrated knife, ready to slice into their delicious labor of love.

With the first cut, a moment of silence enveloped them, each lost in the anticipation of the first bite. Then, as they savored the rich, indulgent flavors, laughter erupted from both of them, filling the kitchen with an infectious joy. "It's perfect!" Sarah exclaimed, her cheeks adorned with smudges of chocolate frosting, a testament to their fun as well as a hint of the delightful chaos that accompanied their baking session.

Emily chuckled softly, brushing a stray hair from Sarah's forehead as she replied with warmth in her voice, "It's not just the cake that's perfect; it's our day together." She pulled her daughter close for a heartfelt hug, the warmth of their time spent together enveloping them like the smell of freshly baked treats. "This was so much more than just baking; it was about creating cherished memories that will last a lifetime." And in that moment, amid the laughter and the sweet aroma of their delightful creation, they both understood that the true magic lay not only in the cake but also in the beautiful bond they had strengthened through their shared experience.

With Stories
LEARNING ENGLISH

Tom, John, and Uncle Ted Go Fishing

Fishing is more than just a leisure activity; it's a cherished tradition, a bonding experience, and an excuse to escape the hustle and bustle of everyday life. For Tom and John, this was precisely the plan when they decided to spend a day on the lake with Uncle Ted, their adventurous and easy-going uncle. This is the story of their memorable fishing trip.

The Early Morning Excitement

The sun had just begun to peek over the horizon, casting a warm golden glow over the landscape. Tom and John woke up early, their excitement palpable as they packed their gear. They loaded a cooler with sandwiches, drinks, and a few snacks, ensuring they were well-prepared for a long, enjoyable day by the water. Uncle Ted arrived shortly after, bringing with him an old tackle box filled with lures and bait that had surely seen many fishing adventures.

"Ready for some fun, boys?" Uncle Ted exclaimed, his energy contagious. As they piled into Uncle Ted's truck, the boys could hardly contain their anticipation. They sang along to classic rock tunes on the radio while Uncle Ted shared tales of his own fishing exploits, embellishing stories with animated gestures and infectious laughter.

Setting Sail

They arrived at the lake by mid-morning, greeted by the sight of shimmering water and the gentle sound of lapping waves. After unloading their gear, Uncle Ted led the boys to his trusty fishing boat. They settled in, and with a turn of the key, the engine roared to life, sending them gliding across the glassy surface of the lake.

"Let's head to that spot by the cove," Uncle Ted suggested. Tom and John nodded eagerly; the cove was rumored to be a hotspot for bass. The ride was filled with shouts of excitement and playful splashes as the boys leaned over the side, trying to catch minnows with their bare hands.

With Stories
LEARNING ENGLISH

Casting Lines and Family Bonding

Once they found a promising spot, Uncle Ted anchored the boat, and the trio prepared their rods. Uncle Ted demonstrated the perfect casting technique, showing Tom and John how to flick their wrists just right to send the bait far into the water. After a few attempts, the boys caught on well and were soon casting their lines with confidence.

As they waited for a bite, Uncle Ted shared wisdom about fishing—talking about patience, the best times to fish, and how to identify different fish species. Tom and John listened intently, soaking up every bit of knowledge their uncle had to offer. They also shared stories of school, friends, and their dreams, the familial bond strengthening with each laugh and shared experience.

A Catch to Remember

Hours passed filled with both patience and anticipation. Finally, Tom felt a tug on his line. "I think I've got something!" he shouted, his excitement echoing across the water. Uncle Ted quickly offered encouragement, reminding him to stay calm and keep the line taut. After a tense few moments, Tom reeled in a beautiful bass, its scales glistening in the sun.

"Wow! That's a nice one!" John cheered, clapping his hands. Proudly, Uncle Ted took a picture of Tom holding his catch, encapsulating a moment that would be cherished for years to come.

Following Tom's success, John soon had his own thrilling experience when he hooked a fish of his own. The two boys took turns reeling in fish throughout the day, eagerly comparing their catches and celebrating each other's successes.

A Perfect Picnic

After a few hours of fishing, they decided to take a break and enjoy their well-earned picnic. Sitting on the boat with the sun warming their faces, they dug into sandwiches and snacks, relishing the flavors and each other's company. Uncle Ted recounted tales of his fishing trips from years past, filling the air with laughter and warmth.

With Stories
LEARNING ENGLISH

The serene view of the lake, the gentle rustling of leaves, and the distant call of birds made for a picturesque setting. It was in moments like these—a shared meal, laughter, and the backdrop of nature—that the boys truly understood the beauty of this day.

Ending the Day on a High Note

As the sun began to dip low in the sky, casting long shadows across the water, it was time to pack up and head back. With a cooler full of fish and hearts full of joy, Tom, John, and Uncle Ted reflected on the day's adventures.

"Thanks for a great day, Uncle Ted!" Tom said, smiling.

"Anytime, boys. Remember, it's not just about the fishing—it's about the memories we create together," Uncle Ted replied, his eyes twinkling.

As they drove home, tired but elated, Tom and John made plans for their next outing. Fishing with Uncle Ted had become more than just a pastime; it was a tradition they would carry on, weaving new stories into the fabric of their family history.

In the end, it was a day filled with laughter, learning, and the joy of family—a perfect fishing trip that neither Tom nor John would soon forget.

As the sun began to dip low in the sky, its warm, golden rays painted the horizon and cast long, playful shadows that danced across the shimmering surface of the water. The tranquil scene was a picturesque backdrop to a day well spent, and as the evening approached, it was clear that it was time to pack up their gear and head back home. With a cooler filled to the brim with the fresh catch of the day and their hearts brimming with joy and satisfaction, Tom, John, and Uncle Ted took a moment to reflect on the day's adventures—each one as vivid and thrilling as the last.

With Stories
LEARNING ENGLISH

"Thanks for a great day, Uncle Ted!" Tom exclaimed, his face glowing with contentment and enthusiasm. He wore a broad smile that mirrored the happiness spilling forth from his heart. The thrill of the fishing expedition, the excitement of the hooks snapping, and the battles with the wriggling fish were like treasures he had captured in his mind.

"Anytime, boys. Remember, it's not just about the fishing—it's about the memories we create together," Uncle Ted replied warmly, his eyes twinkling with wisdom and affection. He leaned back in his seat, cherishing the bond they shared, which was deepened through moments like these. The sagely elder knew that the real prize was not only the fish they caught but the laughter, stories, and connections that would linger long after the lines were cast.

As they drove home, the sun continued its descent, illuminating the road ahead, and the three of them were filled with a comfortable weariness that only comes from a day spent outdoors. Tired yet elated, Tom and John animatedly discussed their next outing, tossing around ideas of new lakes to explore and the ambitious catches they would target. The thrill of anticipation hung in the air as they envisioned future fishing trips, each one likely to be a replay of the joy they experienced today.

Fishing with Uncle Ted had grown to mean so much more than just a casual pastime for the boys; it had evolved into a cherished family tradition, one that they would carry on with pride. Each event was a new thread woven into the fabric of their family history, rich with shared stories that would be recounted for generations to come. In the end, the day was filled with abundant laughter, lessons learned, and the exquisite joy that only family can bring—a perfect fishing trip that neither Tom nor John would soon forget. They knew, deep down, that it was days like these that created unbreakable bonds, moments that would stay with them long after the sun had set and the stars began to twinkle in the night sky. Each adventure held the promise of something magical, and they could hardly wait to cast their lines once more, eager for the next chapter in their family's story.

With Stories
LEARNING ENGLISH

Fishing with Uncle Ted had grown to mean so much more than just a casual pastime for the boys; it had evolved into a cherished family tradition, deeply rooted in love and connection, one that they would carry on with pride. What began as simple outings in search of the perfect catch transformed over the years into a tapestry rich with shared experiences and laughter, each trip adding a new thread into the intricate fabric of their family history. During these outings, they created a wealth of memories that would be recounted for generations to come—stories filled with both hilarity and adventure, laughter ringing out across the water, and moments of quiet reflection shared between brothers.

Each fishing expedition was not just an opportunity to reel in fish but an occasion that fostered deeper bonds among them. As they navigated the scenic rivers and tranquil lakes under the wide-open sky, they shared tales of their lives, exchanged dreams and aspirations, and offered each other advice, all while reeling in their lines with hopeful anticipation. With each sunlit day spent together, the boys absorbed Uncle Ted's wisdom, learning not only the art of fishing but also the principles of patience and perseverance—qualities that would serve them well beyond the boat.

In the end, every trip was filled with abundant laughter, invaluable lessons learned, and the exquisite joy that only family can bring—a perfect fishing day that neither Tom nor John would soon forget. They sat side by side on the edge of the boat, the rays of the setting sun casting a warm glow over the calm waters, as they relished the satisfaction of their day's catch. They knew, deep down, that it was days like these that created unbreakable bonds, moments that would stay with them long after the sun had set and the stars began to twinkle in the night sky. As the cool evening breeze danced through the trees, they felt a deep sense of gratitude for the legacy Uncle Ted had created, a legacy that intertwined their lives in a way that was both palpable and profound.

With Stories
LEARNING ENGLISH

Each adventure held the promise of something magical, a chance to step away from the chaos of everyday life and immerse themselves in the serenity of nature. They could hardly wait to cast their lines once more, hearts swelling with excitement and anticipation for the next chapter in their family's story—each trip a new page, rich with potential and endless possibilities, as they continued to weave their lives together under the vast, starry sky. The simple act of fishing had transformed into a celebration of family, a reminder of what truly mattered: the love they shared and the lasting memories they were creating together.

With Stories
LEARNING ENGLISH

Alex's Morning Routine

As dawn broke, casting a soft golden hue through the curtains, Alex stirred awake. The crisp morning air whispered promises of a new day, and after a brief moment of stretching and shaking off the remnants of sleep, he swung his legs over the side of the bed. It was time to embrace the morning.

Rising to the Daylight

After a refreshing splash of cold water on his face, Alex felt invigorated and ready to tackle the day ahead. He opened the window, allowing the gentle breeze to flow in, carrying with it the fresh scents of grass and blooming flowers. In the distance, he could hear birds chirping, adding a melodic backdrop to the quiet morning.

With the morning sun turning the world into a canvas of vibrant colors, Alex headed to the kitchen, the heart of his home. The first order of business: breakfast. He believed that starting the day with a good meal set the tone for productivity.

The Breakfast Ritual

Today, he decided to whip up one of his favorite breakfasts: avocado toast topped with a perfectly poached egg. First, he took a ripe avocado, slicing it open to reveal its creamy, green interior. As he mashed it with a sprinkle of salt and a dash of lime juice, the aroma filled the kitchen, making his stomach rumble with anticipation.

While the water on the stove came to a gentle boil, he pulled out two slices of whole-grain bread, placing them in the toaster. The sound of the toaster popping up was a familiar and comforting notification that breakfast was close at hand.

With practiced ease, he carefully lowered an egg into the simmering water, watching as it began to cook. The moments felt tranquil—the clattering of pots, the bubbling water, and the faint sizzle of bread browning created a symphony of morning sounds that Alex had come to cherish.

With Stories
LEARNING ENGLISH

Savoring the Moment

Once everything was ready, Alex plated his creation, placing the vibrant green avocado mash on the toasted bread and delicately placing the poached egg on top. A dusting of chili flakes and a sprinkle of freshly chopped herbs added a touch of color and zest. He couldn't wait to dig in.

Seated at his small kitchen table, he sipped on a steaming cup of coffee while admiring the beautiful view of the garden just outside his window. The simple act of savoring his breakfast became a ritual of mindfulness. As he took each bite, he relished the flavors, appreciating the effort he put into the morning meal.

A Moment of Reflection

Breakfast wasn't just about fuel for Alex; it was a moment of reflection. He used this time to go over his plans for the day. With a full heart and an optimistic mind, he considered the challenges and opportunities that lay ahead. Whether it was a meeting at work or a simple task like organizing his space, he believed that each moment could be met with enthusiasm.

As he finished his meal, feeling satisfied and energized, he cleared the table and rinsed the dishes. The morning sun now streamed brightly through the window, a reminder of the importance of new beginnings. With a renewed sense of purpose, Alex was ready to step out into the world and make the most of the day.

In Conclusion

Alex's morning routine was more than just waking up and having breakfast; it was a series of mindful choices that set a positive tone for the day. In that simple act of preparing and enjoying breakfast, he found a moment of peace amidst the hustle and bustle of everyday life. And as he ventured out, he carried with him the warmth of the morning's embrace, ready to face whatever challenges awaited him.

With Stories
LEARNING ENGLISH

The familiar feelings of excitement and urgency washed over him; a new day at work awaited, filled with both opportunities and challenges.

After tidying up the kitchen and giving his apartment one last once-over, Alex grabbed his backpack, making sure he had everything he needed for the day ahead—his laptop, a notebook, and the all-important coffee thermos. He glanced at the clock on the wall; it was time to head out.

Stepping out of his cozy home, Alex was greeted by the fresh morning air. He took a moment to appreciate the stillness of the neighborhood before it fully awakened. Birds chirped happily in the trees, and the faint sound of distant traffic began to build. He locked the door behind him and set off toward the bus stop, his footsteps crunching on the gravel path.

Alex's daily commute involved catching the bus, a routine he had perfected over the years. He found solace in the predictability of the bus schedule and the companionship of fellow commuters. As he walked, he thought about the projects awaiting him at the office, his mind racing through the tasks he hoped to accomplish.

Arriving at the bus stop, Alex saw a few familiar faces. A young woman was engrossed in her book, while an elderly man was consulting his smartphone, likely checking the bus arrival times. As they exchanged nods and friendly smiles, Alex felt a sense of community among the diverse group of riders. These small connections brought warmth to his mornings, and he often wondered about the stories behind each of their lives.

The bus arrived with a whoosh, its doors swinging open in welcome. Alex boarded, swiping his transit card and making his way to an empty seat by the window. As the bus pulled away from the curb, he settled in, watching the world zip by. The rhythmic sound of the bus engine was soothing; he opened his laptop for a moment to review his agenda, but found his gaze drifting outside.

The streets were alive with activity. He observed people walking their dogs, others jogging past, and a few children bundled up with their parents, ready for school. Each glimpse was a tiny reminder of life's hustle and bustle. Alex felt grateful for this moment of reflection—an opportunity to mentally prepare for the day and appreciate the little things that often went unnoticed amid the chaos of daily routines.

With Stories
LEARNING ENGLISH

As the bus navigated through the city, Alex caught up on messages and emails on his phone. He used these fleeting minutes to stay connected with colleagues and friends, knowing full well how valuable time could be. The world outside transformed as they traveled further into the heart of the city; tall buildings replaced the residential areas, showcasing a vibrant urban landscape.

Finally, the bus approached his stop, and Alex gathered his things, ready for another fulfilling day at work. He stepped off the bus, taking a deep breath of the crisp city air as he bid farewell to his fellow passengers. With a wave to the bus driver, he began his walk to the office, feeling a renewed sense of purpose.

Despite the mundane nature of his commute, Alex found joy in the routine. It was more than just a means to get from Point A to Point B; it was a moment of connection, reflection, and preparation for everything life had in store. With each step towards his workplace, Alex reminded himself that every day was an opportunity—an opportunity to learn, grow, and make a difference.

As he entered the office building, the hustle and bustle around him grew more pronounced, but Alex embraced it, ready to dive into another workday filled with potential. And while his journey began with a simple breakfast at home and a bus ride, it was these small moments that truly shaped his day.

It was an ordinary Wednesday morning when Alex stepped into the office, the familiar sights and sounds greeting him like an old friend. The soft hum of computers, the rustle of papers, and the gentle chatter of colleagues set the backdrop for yet another day of productivity. But for Alex, this day held the promise of something more—something that made his heart skip a beat.

As he settled into his workstation, his thoughts drifted to Sarah, the girl who had unknowingly ensnared his heart. She was the kind of person who could light up a room with her laughter and warmth. They worked in the same department but often found themselves engaged in casual conversations that lingered long after meetings had concluded. Each smile exchanged and each shared joke deepened his affection for her, igniting a spark that Alex hoped could eventually glow into something more.

With Stories
LEARNING ENGLISH

Today was no ordinary day; it was the day Alex had decided to muster up the courage to express his feelings for Sarah. With every task he completed—reviewing reports, answering emails, and attending meetings—his mind buzzed with thoughts about how he could approach her. Should he ask her to lunch? Or perhaps invite her to join him for Friday's office happy hour? The possibilities felt endless, yet the weight of uncertainty loomed over him.

As the clock ticked closer to noon, Alex found his heart racing. He glanced over at Sarah, who was focused on her screen, a hint of concentration furrowing her brow. In that moment, he saw not just a colleague but the potential for a deeper connection. He took a deep breath, his resolve strengthening. If he was going to take this leap, now was the time.

Gathering his thoughts, Alex walked over to Sarah's desk. "Hey, do you have a minute?" he asked, trying to keep his voice steady. She looked up, her eyes sparkling with curiosity. "Of course! What's up?" As they chatted, Alex felt a surge of confidence wash over him. They discussed plans for the upcoming weekend, and as conversations turned to hobbies and interests, he couldn't help but admire her passion for photography. That interest, combined with her radiant personality, was the perfect blend that had him utterly captivated. "Actually," Alex began, feeling the butterflies in his stomach, "I was wondering if you'd like to grab lunch with me today. I've been meaning to ask you!" The moment hung in the air, and for a split second, he feared he had misread the signs.

A bright smile broke across Sarah's face, illuminating her features. "I'd love that! I was hoping you'd ask," she replied, her excitement palpable.

The relief flooded through Alex, and as they agreed on a time to meet at the café down the street, he felt as if a weight had been lifted from his shoulders.

As the day progressed and they shared laughs over sandwiches and salads, Alex realized just how much he treasured these moments—each conversation, every shared smile. He discovered that Sarah was not only intelligent and witty but also deeply caring, and with each exchange, the bond between them grew stronger.

With Stories
LEARNING ENGLISH

By the time they returned to the office, Alex felt as though something had shifted. The lines between colleagues and friends blurred into something more significant. As the days turned into weeks, their friendship flourished, filled with laughter, shared goals, and aspirations for the future.

In an environment often focused on deadlines and deliverables, Alex's heart found a new rhythm against the backdrop of work. Love had indeed bloomed amid office walls, transforming his daily grind into something extraordinary. As they continued to navigate their professional lives, Alex cherished the journey he and Sarah were on—a journey that began with a simple 'hello' and blossomed into an inspiring romance, proving that sometimes love truly does find a way, even in the busiest of places.

With every lingering glance and shared joke, Alex knew that he had embarked on a beautiful adventure, one that had changed his perspective on both love and work forever.

With Stories
LEARNING ENGLISH

By the time they returned to the office, Alex sensed a subtle yet profound shift in the dynamics around him. The previously distinct lines separating colleagues from friends had begun to merge, evolving into something far more meaningful. As the days stretched into weeks, the bond between Alex and Sarah flourished, blossoming with the sweetness of laughter, the excitement of shared goals, and the promise of aspirations that reached far beyond the confines of their office cubicles.

In a workplace that typically prioritized deadlines and deliverables, Alex found himself caught in a whirlwind of emotions. His heart had discovered a new rhythm, one that pulsed joyfully against the often monotonous backdrop of work life. Love had, against all odds, begun to bloom within the very fabric of the office, imbuing his daily grind with an extraordinary vibrancy that he had never anticipated. The long hours spent together discussing projects were now accompanied by stolen glances and spark-filled conversations, each moment piling up like treasured memories, transforming the mundane into the miraculous.

As the duo expertly navigated their professional responsibilities side by side, Alex found himself cherishing not only the tasks at hand but the beautiful journey he and Sarah were embarking on together. What had started as a simple 'hello' had blossomed into an inspiring romance, reminding him of the magic that life could hold, even in the midst of a demanding workplace. It was a testament to the idea that sometimes, love truly does find a way, even in the busiest of places, like the bustling office where they spent so many hours. Each lingering gaze shared across the conference table, each inside joke exchanged during coffee breaks, reinforced Alex's understanding that he had embarked on a beautiful and transformative adventure. The experience had reshaped his outlook on both love and work, intertwining the two aspects of his life in a manner he had never imagined was possible. With Sarah by his side, work had become not just a duty but a canvas filled with colors of affection and companionship, one that promised to render each day an exciting chapter in this unexpected love story.

With Stories
LEARNING ENGLISH

Two Friends at the Concert of a Lifetime

Concerts hold a special place in the hearts of music lovers, creating unforgettable memories that linger long after the last note fades away. This essence of shared experience is vividly captured in the story of two friends, Mia and Zoe, as they embark on a magical night filled with music, laughter, and adventure.

The Anticipation Builds

Months of planning and excitement had led up to this unforgettable evening. Mia and Zoe, both avid music fans, had been eagerly awaiting the day they would see their favorite band perform live. The announcement of the concert had brought squeals of delight and numerous late-night discussions about setlists, outfits, and everything in between. The day before the concert, they charged their phones for capturing moments, made playlists for the drive, and even practiced their favorite lyrics together.

As the day of the concert arrived, the air buzzed with anticipation. The friends donned matching band t-shirts and glittery accessories, excited to express their fandom while capturing the attention of fellow concert-goers. The drive to the venue was filled with the music they loved, each song a reminder of the countless memories tied to it—from late-night sing-alongs to road trips with the windows down.

Arrival at the Venue

Upon arriving at the venue, the girls were greeted by an electrifying atmosphere. Fans of all ages filled the parking lot, wearing merchandise from past tours, sharing their excitement, and indulging in pre-concert rituals. The smell of food trucks wafted through the air, enticing attendees to grab a bite before the show. Mia and Zoe spent the time dancing to street performers and capturing candid photos that encapsulated their bubbling excitement.

As the doors opened, the crowd surged forward, and they found their place close to the stage—an ideal spot to experience the music up close. Surrounded by passionate fans, they felt the collective energy build as the opening act took the stage. They cheered and sang along, already caught up in the rhythm of the night.

With Stories
LEARNING ENGLISH

The Main Event
When the headlining band finally took the stage, the roar of the crowd was deafening. The lights flashed, and the music surged through the speakers, washing over Mia and Zoe like a wave of pure joy. They danced and sang as the band launched into its biggest hits, their voices blending into the symphony of the audience. In that moment, nothing else mattered; it was just them, the music, and thousands of kindred spirits united by their love of the band.

The girls found themselves lost in the music, each song awakening memories of friends, summer nights, and cherished moments. They laughed freely, shared snacks, and even made new friends in the crowd.

As the band played their favorite song, a ballad that spoke to their friendship, they locked eyes and sang into the night, feeling the lyrics reverberate through their souls.

A Surprise Encounter
As if the night wasn't already perfect, a delightful surprise awaited them. During a break between songs, the frontman of the band noticed a sign held aloft by a fan even farther up front, reading, "Best friends since kindergarten!" He paused, acknowledging the friendship and inviting the girls to share their story. Before they knew it, Mia and Zoe had made it onto the big screen, jumping up and down with pure

exhilaration as the crowd cheered for them. It was a moment that would forever be etched in their memories.

The Aftermath

As the concert drew to a close, the girls tried to hold on to every last moment. They exchanged glances of disbelief and glee, knowing they had just experienced something remarkable. When the final chord was struck, confetti rained down from above, marking the end of a night filled with dreams fulfilled.

Driving home under a canopy of stars, Mia and Zoe reflected on the evening—the conversations, the music, and the memories etched into their hearts. The night had solidified their bond, reminding them of the importance of friendship and shared experiences.

With Stories
LEARNING ENGLISH

Concerts have an extraordinary way of bringing people together and creating unbreakable bonds. For Mia and Zoe, this night wasn't just about the music; it was a testament to their friendship, a night they would cherish forever. As they made their promises to attend many more concerts together, they knew that wherever life took them, the rhythm of that unforgettable night would always play in their hearts. As the concert drew to a close, the atmosphere was electric, buzzing with the echoes of the unforgettable performance. The girls, Mia and Zoe, clung to each fleeting moment, fully aware that they were parting ways with an experience that would linger in their minds for years to come. They exchanged glances filled with disbelief and unbridled glee, their eyes sparkling with the thrill of having witnessed something that felt larger than life. The music had swept them away; every note, every harmony, had woven itself intricately into the fabric of their friendship.

When the final chord was struck, the venue erupted in applause, and just then, as if timed perfectly, cascades of colorful confetti rained down from above, transforming the stage into a vibrant spectacle of joy. This was not just the end of a concert; it was the concluding act of a night that had been a journey of dreams fulfilled and moments savored. Surrounded by cheering fans, the girls embraced the sudden shower of festivity, feeling as if the universe was celebrating their shared passion.

Driving home under a vast canopy of stars that sparkled like diamonds sprinkled across the black velvet sky, Mia and Zoe began to reflect on the evening's magic. The car filled with laughter and reminiscences as they discussed their favorite moments from the show—the thrilling crescendo of a beloved song, the exhilaration shared in the crowd, the spontaneous dance moves they couldn't help but unleash. Each conversation was a thread, delicately weaving the night's highlights into the tapestry of their lives, those memories now etched permanently in their hearts.

The night had not only entertained them but had also solidified their bond, a potent reminder of the importance of friendship and the power of shared experiences. They shared how moments like these, bursting with excitement and camaraderie, were essential in a world that could often feel disconnected. Concerts have an extraordinary way of binding people together, transcending the ordinary and creating unbreakable bonds.

With Stories
LEARNING ENGLISH

For Mia and Zoe, this particular night was not just about the music; it was a beautiful testament to their enduring friendship. They reminisced about all the times they had supported each other and celebrated together, and they knew this night would be a cherished memory they would hold close to their hearts for years to come. As they made heartfelt promises to attend many more concerts and create new memories in the future, they realized something profound: no matter where life might lead them or what challenges lay ahead, the rhythm of that unforgettable night—the exhilarating

With Stories
LEARNING ENGLISH

music and the joyous atmosphere—would always play in their hearts, a cherished soundtrack of their friendship. For Mia and Zoe, this particular night was not just about the music; it was a beautiful testament to their enduring friendship, a vibrant mosaic woven together by laughter, shared secrets, and countless unforgettable moments. As the sun dipped below the horizon, painting the sky in hues of orange and pink, they found themselves surrounded by the pulsing energy of the crowd, feeling an electric anticipation swell in the air.

They reminisced about all the times they had supported each other through thick and thin—those late-night phone calls when life felt overwhelming, the spontaneous adventures that led to unexpected stories, and the quiet moments of comfort when words were unnecessary. Each memory they shared was a stepping stone on the path of their friendship, a reminder of how they had celebrated each other's victories, no matter how small, and held each other up during times of despair.

As the first notes of the concert spilled into the warm night, infusing them with an infectious energy, they knew that this night would be a cherished memory they would hold close to their hearts for years to come. With every beat, the music wrapped around them, pulling them deeper into the moment, and they felt an overwhelming sense of gratitude. They shared smiles and laughter, their voices rising above the music as they declared heartfelt promises to attend many more concerts and create new memories in the future.

In that lively atmosphere, surrounded by fellow fans lost in the music, they realized something profound: no matter where life might lead them or what challenges lay ahead, the rhythm of that unforgettable night—the exhilarating music, the joyous atmosphere, and the warmth of each other's presence—would always play in their hearts. It would become a cherished soundtrack of their friendship, a melody that underscored their shared experiences, reminding them that they were never alone in life's journey.

With Stories
LEARNING ENGLISH

As the night wore on, with each song echoing their excitement and every cheer reinforcing their bond, Mia and Zoe felt an unspoken assurance that their friendship would withstand the test of time. They danced freely under the stars, letting the music guide them, reveling in the knowledge that this night was one of many beautiful chapters in their story—a story that was still being written, filled with the promise of new adventures and the enduring love that only true friends can share.

With a powerful car beneath him, meticulously engineered for speed and agility, an exceptional team working tirelessly in the pits, meticulously strategizing and executing each pit stop with precision, and an indomitable spirit that refuses to waver in the face of adversity, the odds appear to favor him in this high-stakes competition. The atmosphere is electric, charged with anticipation and excitement, as supporters and pundits alike share a genuine sense of optimism. There is a strong belief among fans and experts alike that not only could Fred clinch the championship title—the pinnacle of achievement in this thrilling sport—but he could also etch his name alongside the legends whose feats have inspired countless aspiring racers throughout history. Every turn he takes on the circuit, every lap he completes with breathtaking finesse, and every precious second spent on the track brings him exponentially closer to the realization of his lifelong dreams. The roar of the crowd fuels his determination, pushing him to excel beyond his limits. The world watches breathlessly as he races toward his destiny, following every twist and turn of his journey with rapt attention. The stakes have never been higher, and the tension is palpable as each race unfolds, revealing the fierce competition and showcasing Fred's unwavering resolve. This is a moment that transcends mere sport; it represents the culmination of years of hard work, sacrifice, and relentless passion that Fred has poured into his craft. As he navigates the curves of the track and accelerates toward the finish line, he carries not only his ambitions but also the hopes of fans who believe that they are witnessing something truly extraordinary—a potential legacy in the making.

With Stories
LEARNING ENGLISH

The Rising Star of Racing with His Championship-Worthy Car

As the engines roar and tires screech around the racetrack, one name keeps buzzing among fans and fellow competitors alike: Fred. With the season nearing its conclusion, there is an undeniable excitement surging through the racing community, fueled by Fred's remarkable performances and his high-octane machine. Many are ready to call it now — Fred will be the next champion, and his car is the reason why.

A Perfect Match: Fred and His Race Car

From the moment Fred slid into the cockpit of his sleek, aerodynamic race car, something magical happened. Built for speed, agility, and precision, his vehicle represents cutting-edge engineering and an undying passion for racing. With a lightweight chassis design for optimal handling and a powerful engine that screams down the straightaways, this car is the perfect extension of Fred's racing prowess. But it's not just the car; it's how Fred drives it. Known for his strategic mind, Fred has a knack for reading the track and anticipating his competitors' moves. Whether he's slipping past an opponent on a tight bend or expertly managing tire wear to stretch his pit stops, Fred's tactical brilliance elevates the performance of his vehicle, giving him an edge when it matters most.

The Road to Glory

Fred's journey to becoming a champion has not been easy. He faced setbacks, including mechanical failures, fierce competition, and moments of self-doubt. Yet, with each obstacle, Fred has emerged stronger. His resilience has inspired his team and fans, and that spirit is reflected in every lap he completes.

This season, Fred has consistently finished at the top, boasting several podium finishes that have catapulted him into the championship conversation. His fans, who have loyally followed his journey, now wear his merchandise with pride, confident that this year is the year they will celebrate his crowning moment.

With Stories
LEARNING ENGLISH

Behind the Scenes: Teamwork and Innovation

While Fred's talent shines on the track, it's essential to acknowledge the dedicated team working tirelessly behind the scenes. From engineers to pit crew, every member plays a vital role in refining Fred's vehicle and supporting his quest for championship glory.

With advanced technology, they continuously optimize the car's performance, making adjustments based on each performance data. The synergy between Fred and his team ensures that the car not only meets the challenges of the race but beats them.

The Final Countdown

As the season enters its final stretch, the anticipation is palpable. With each race, the stakes grow higher, and the pressure intensifies. But Fred remains unfazed. He acknowledges the pressure but channels it into motivation, focusing on what he can control: his driving, his preparation, and his determination to claim the title.

Fans and analysts alike eagerly await the upcoming championship races. Will Fred cross the finish line first and secure his place in racing history? With his car, his team, and his unyielding spirit, there's a strong possibility that not only will he claim the championship but also solidify his legacy as one of the sport's greats.

As the racing season draws near its climax, an electric sense of anticipation fills the air. Each passing race elevates the thrill, with increasing stakes that cast a heavier burden of expectation on the drivers. The ambiance is charged with a mix of excitement and anxiety as fans, teams, and pundits alike look forward to the upcoming events. Among all the competitors, Fred stands out, embodying a calm resolve that seems almost otherworldly in the face of growing pressure.

With Stories
LEARNING ENGLISH

While many around him may feel the weight of expectation bearing down, Fred accepts this tension as a part of the sport. Rather than letting it overwhelm him, he skillfully transforms it into a source of motivation that propels him forward. He remains focused on the facets of the competition he can influence: honing his driving skills, meticulously preparing for each race, and nurturing the unshakeable determination that has brought him to this pivotal moment in his career. In Fred's eyes, the championship title is not just a trophy; it represents a culmination of hard work, talent, and unrelenting ambition.

As the championship races loom on the horizon, fans can hardly contain their excitement. Analysts pore over statistics, dissecting Fred's past performances while speculating on the challenges that lie ahead.

Questions swirl in the air: Will Fred navigate the courses with the same precision and skill that have defined his driving style? Will he be able to fend off challengers who are just as hungry for glory? Will he, at long last, cross the finish line first and secure his rightful place in the annals of racing history?

With a powerful car beneath him, an exceptional team working tirelessly in the pits, and an indomitable spirit that refuses to waver in the face of adversity, the odds appear to favor him. There is a genuine sense among fans and experts that not only could Fred clinch the championship, but he could also etch his name alongside the legends of the sport. Every turn, every lap, and every second on the track brings him closer to the realization of his dreams, and the world watches breathlessly as he races towards destiny.

With Stories
LEARNING ENGLISH

With a powerful car beneath him, meticulously engineered for speed and agility, an exceptional team working tirelessly in the pits, meticulously strategizing and executing each pit stop with precision, and an indomitable spirit that refuses to waver in the face of adversity, the odds appear to favor him in this high-stakes competition. The atmosphere is electric, charged with anticipation and excitement, as supporters and pundits alike share a genuine sense of optimism. There is a strong belief among fans and experts alike that not only could Fred clinch the championship title—the pinnacle of achievement in this thrilling sport—but he could also etch his name alongside the legends whose feats have inspired countless aspiring racers throughout history.

Every turn he takes on the circuit, every lap he completes with breathtaking finesse, and every precious second spent on the track brings him exponentially closer to the realization of his lifelong dreams. The roar of the crowd fuels his determination, pushing him to excel beyond his limits. The world watches breathlessly as he races toward his destiny, following every twist and turn of his journey with rapt attention. The stakes have never been higher, and the tension is palpable as each race unfolds, revealing the fierce competition and showcasing Fred's unwavering resolve. This is a moment that transcends mere sport; it represents the culmination of years of hard work, sacrifice, and relentless passion that Fred has poured into his craft. As he navigates the curves of the track and accelerates toward the finish line, he carries not only his ambitions but also the hopes of fans who believe that they are witnessing something truly extraordinary—a potential legacy in the making.

With Stories
LEARNING ENGLISH

The Day a Thief Targeted a Local Bank

On an ordinary Wednesday morning, the quiet hum of a small town bank was shattered by an unexpected turn of events. What should have been a routine day for both employees and customers became a scene straight out of a thriller when a thief entered the bank with a plan that would lead to a tense confrontation.

The Setup

As sunlight streamed through the bank's windows, casting a warm glow, inside, the atmosphere was calm. Julie, a pregnant cashier at the bank, had just started her shift. For her, the day was laced with excitement and nerves, not just because she was nearing the end of her pregnancy but also because she was about to embark on a new chapter in her life. Little did she know that her day was about to take a dramatic turn.

Meanwhile, a thief—let's call him Jason—was planning his heist. He had meticulously chosen this bank, knowing it appeared quiet and lacked robust security measures. Desperation drove his actions. Broke and frustrated with his circumstances, he felt he had no other options. He thought about the swift payoff, imagining the bills he would collect, but he didn't foresee the chaotic confrontation that would ensue.

The Heist Unfolds

Jason breached the bank's doors, his heart racing as he pulled a bandana over his face. Glancing around, he assessed the situation—two tellers, a couple of customers, and the bank manager in his office. He approached Julie's counter, his demeanor intimidating.

With Stories
LEARNING ENGLISH

"Give me all the cash in your drawer," he ordered, his voice shaking slightly but laced with urgency. Julie's eyes widened, and for a moment, time stood still. The pregnant cashier felt a surge of fear ripple through her; her mind raced with thoughts of her unborn child. Though she was terrified, Julie remained composed. With trembling hands, she reached into her drawer, but a cascade of thoughts flooded her mind. What if he's armed? What if he gets violent? She glimpsed the reflection of other bank employees in the glass behind her, trying to signal them to remain calm.

A Moment of Courage

In that moment, something shifted within Julie. Though fear coursed through her veins, she knew she had to remain strong—for herself and her unborn child. Taking a deep breath, she said, "Please, just take what you need and leave. No one has to get hurt."

Her calmness seemed to surprise Jason, if only for a moment. He paused, his expression softening slightly as he stared into her worried eyes. For a brief second, he hesitated, caught between his instincts and the weight of the situation.

Suddenly, the bank manager, alerted by the tension in the air, made a quiet move towards the panic button hidden under his desk. Unbeknownst to Jason, help was on the way, and that split-second hesitation would become his undoing.

The Aftermath

Within minutes, sirens echoed through the streets, growing louder as police arrived on the scene. In a panic, Jason made a run for it. But outside, the police had set up a perimeter, and he soon found himself cornered.

As chaos unfolded, Julie waited anxiously, clutching her belly, grateful that she had remained composed during the ordeal. The incident concluded with Jason's arrest, and thankfully, no one was hurt. However, the emotional toll on the bank employees and customers lingered long after the sirens faded.

With Stories
LEARNING ENGLISH

Within mere moments of the chaos erupting, the wailing of sirens pierced the tranquil backdrop of the quiet town, reverberating through the streets and growing increasingly louder as law enforcement officers rushed to the scene. Panic set in for Jason, who instinctively decided to make a run for it, driven by an overwhelming sense of fear and desperation. As he hurriedly fled the bank, adrenaline coursing through his veins, he was blissfully unaware of the meticulous planning that the police had put in place. Outside, officers had swiftly established a perimeter, blocking all potential escape routes, and before he knew it, Jason found himself trapped, caught between his hasty decision and the law closing in around him.

Meanwhile, amid the turmoil unfolding just a few blocks away, Julie anxiously awaited any updates, her heart pounding as she clutched her growing belly. As an expectant mother, she felt a mixture of fear and gratitude; grateful that she had remained composed throughout the ordeal, managing to protect not only herself but also the life she carried within her. Each passing moment felt like an eternity as she replayed the events in her mind, trying to understand how a routine day at the bank had turned into a scene of chaos.

The incident culminated in Jason's arrest, a sobering conclusion to an afternoon that had spiraled completely out of control. Fortunately, amidst the chaos and confusion, no one was physically harmed during the incident. Yet, as the blaring sirens began to fade into the distance and the police presence shifted to cleanup and investigation, the emotional scars left on the bank's employees and customers continued to resonate long after the external tumult had dissipated.

With Stories
LEARNING ENGLISH

Those who had been part of the frightening experience experienced a lingering sense of unease, grappling with the trauma of what had transpired. Employees shared worried glances, their laughter replaced by hushed conversations, while customers left the bank with heavy hearts, shaken by the unpredictability of violence. Julie, despite her relief at the outcome, knew that the psychological impact would linger, like a shadow that follows long after the lights of a crisis have dimmed. The community would have to band together in the days and weeks that followed, supporting one another as they navigated the aftermath—not just of an event, but of a collective trauma that would forever alter their sense of safety and normalcy.

Those who had been part of the frightening experience—an event that had thrust them into a whirlwind of chaos and uncertainty—found themselves grappling with a lingering sense of unease that clung to them like an unwelcome shroud. They faced the daunting task of coming to terms with the trauma of what had transpired, with echoes of fear replaying in their minds. In the days that followed, employees exchanged worried glances, recognizing the shared weight of their experience. The atmosphere, once filled with vibrant laughter and camaraderie, was now permeated by a heavy silence, as humor was replaced with quiet, hushed conversations that reflected their shared anxiety.

Meanwhile, customers left the bank with heavy hearts, their spirits deeply shaken by the unpredictability and brutality of violence that had invaded what was supposed to be a routine day. Each person carried the emotional scars of that moment, a stark reminder of how quickly normalcy could be uprooted. Julie, despite her undeniable relief at the outcome—grateful that no lives had been lost and that the immediate danger had passed—was acutely aware that the psychological impact of such an event would linger long after the crisis had subsided. It was akin to a shadow that trailed behind, an omnipresent reminder of an ordeal that had threatened their sense of security.

In this fragile state, the community faced the urgent need to come together in the days and weeks that lay ahead. They understood that they must support one another, cultivating a shared resilience as they navigated the turbulent aftermath. This was not merely a response to an isolated event; it was about confronting the pervasive effects

With Stories
LEARNING ENGLISH

of a collective trauma that would forever change their perception of safety and normalcy. As they rebuilt their lives, the bonds forged in this experience would become their anchor, guiding them through the emotional landscape that lay ahead, fostering a sense of solidarity and hope even in the darkest of times.

In this delicate and fragile state of existence, the community found itself grappling with profound challenges. The urgency to unite loomed large in the days and weeks that followed the distressing event, creating a pressing need for togetherness and mutual support. They recognized that in order to heal and move forward, they must stand as one, cultivating a shared resilience that would help them navigate the turbulent aftermath of their collective ordeal.

This effort was not simply a reaction to an isolated incident; rather, it represented a concerted effort to confront the pervasive, often insidious effects of a collective trauma that had infiltrated their lives. The trauma they experienced extended beyond the boundaries of the specific event—it was an unsettling force that reshaped their perception of safety, security, and what they once considered normal. The very fabric of their community was shaken, leaving them acutely aware of fragility amidst life's unpredictability.

As they began the painstaking process of rebuilding their lives, the bonds that were formed in the crucible of this shared experience proved to be invaluable. These connections, strengthened through empathy, understanding, and shared sorrow, became their anchor. They provided the stability and support needed to navigate the emotional landscape that lay ahead, a landscape marked by uncertainty, fear, and grief. Yet, within this daunting terrain, the community also discovered the seeds of solidarity and hope.

As they leaned on one another, they realized that their shared journey, although filled with challenges, could also be a source of strength and resilience. Listening to each other's stories, offering comfort and companionship, and engaging in acts of kindness were essential components of their healing process. Together, they fostered an environment where vulnerability was met with compassion, allowing individuals to express their fears and anxieties without judgment.

With Stories
LEARNING ENGLISH

Even in the darkest of times, as they journeyed through the waves of sorrow and uncertainty, they found moments of light. Laughter erupted in the most unexpected places, small acts of kindness bloomed amidst despair, and the sense of community persevered. Each gathering, each shared meal, and each moment of togetherness became a testament to their determination to emerge from the shadows of trauma stronger than before. In this profound journey of healing, they not only rebuilt their physical lives but also rekindled their hopes and dreams. What emerged from the ashes of tragedy was not merely a fractured community; instead, it was a resilient collective equipped with the understanding that healing is a shared journey—a testament to the power of unity in facing adversity. Through every challenge they encountered, the bonds they forged would guide them, helping them to rise above the pain and to reimagine a future infused with possibility, compassion, and unwavering hope.

With Stories
LEARNING ENGLISH

The Adventures of Lila and Mia: The Enchanted Forest

Introduction

Sisters share a bond that transcends time and space, often leading them on remarkable adventures that strengthen their relationship and ignite their imaginations. Lila and Mia, two spirited sisters, found themselves embarking on a whimsical journey like no other, one that would test their courage, strengthen their trust in one another, and unveil the magic hidden within their backyard.

Chapter 1: The Mysterious Map

One sunny afternoon, Lila, the older sister with a wild imagination, was rummaging through the attic of their old house. Among dusty boxes and forgotten toys, she stumbled upon an ornate, weather-beaten chest. Curiosity piqued, she opened it to find a tattered map, yellowed with age. The map depicted their familiar surroundings, but with one curious addition—a marked path leading to an area labeled "The Enchanted Forest."

Excited, Lila rushed to find Mia, her younger sister, who was busy assembling a model of the solar system in her room. "Mia! You won't believe what I found!" Lila exclaimed, holding up the map with sheer exhilaration.

Mia looked up, her eyes sparkling with intrigue. "What is it?"

"It's a treasure map! It leads to the Enchanted Forest!" Lila replied, bouncing on her toes. Always ready for adventure, Mia's interest was piqued.

"Let's go find it!" she exclaimed, setting aside her project.

With Stories
LEARNING ENGLISH

Into the Enchanted Forest

With the map in hand and a backpack filled with snacks and a flashlight, Lila and Mia set off on their journey. They followed the map as they entered a familiar path that curled around the old oak tree in their backyard. But as they walked deeper into the woods, the atmosphere transformed—sunlight filtered through a quilt of oversized leaves, and the air was perfumed with wildflowers.

"It feels magical here," Mia breathed, her eyes wide with wonder.

After trekking for some time, they reached an archway formed by intertwining branches adorned with vibrant flowers. With a shared glance of excitement and determination, they stepped through the arch, unaware that they were crossing the threshold into the enchanted realm.

The Talking Animals

Inside the forest, they were greeted not only by the musical carousel of birds but also by animated creatures. A wise old owl named Orion perched high on a branch.

"Welcome, travelers! Not many find their way to the Enchanted Forest," he hooted. "You must have a purpose to be here."

Lila took a deep breath, "We're searching for a treasure marked on this map."

Orion's eyes twinkled. "Ah, the Treasure of Friendship! You'll need more than just bravery. Solve the riddle of the forest to find it."

Mia, known for her problem-solving skills, stepped forward. "What's the riddle?"

"Listen closely," Orion said. "I speak without a mouth and hear without ears. I have no body, but I come alive with the wind. What am I?"

The sisters pondered. After a moment, Mia's face lit up. "An echo!"

"Very good!" Orion replied, flying down to reveal a hidden path illuminated by soft glowing mushrooms.

With Stories
LEARNING ENGLISH

The Test of Trust

As they followed the new path, they were faced with challenges that tested their bond. The path split into two. One side led to a shimmering lake, while the other delved into the shadows of thick trees.

"I feel we should go to the lake," Mia suggested, drawn by its sparkling allure.

"But the map shows the treasure is hidden deeper in the forest," Lila insisted. "We need to stick to the path."

After a moment of silence filled with doubt, Mia took a deep breath, "I trust you, Lila. Let's follow the map together."

Their mutual trust deepened, and with hands held tightly, they ventured down the shadowed path. Soon, they arrived at a massive ancient tree with a door carved into its trunk.

The Treasure of Friendship

Inside the tree, they found a small chest illuminated by the flickering light of fireflies. They opened it together, revealing not gold or jewels but a collection of shimmering stones—each emblazoned with memories they had shared.

"This isn't just a treasure; it's a reminder of our adventures," Lila said, tears of joy glistening in her eyes.

Mia smiled, her heart swelling with love for her sister. "It's about the journey... and us."

With Stories
LEARNING ENGLISH

As they hugged, the forest seemed to come alive, with flowers blooming and the creatures celebrating their friendship. Orion swooped down, giving them a knowing nod. "You have discovered the true treasure—a bond so strong that it can light up even the darkest paths."

Conclusion

Lila and Mia emerged from the Enchanted Forest hand in hand, forever changed by their adventure. They realized that while paths may lure them with shiny distractions, the true magic lies in the love and trust shared between sisters. With hearts full of joy and pockets brimming with shimmering stones, they returned home, ready for their next adventure—because life is, after all, the greatest adventure of all.

With Stories
LEARNING ENGLISH

A Family Tradition to Savor

On a sunlit Sunday morning, the aroma of freshly brewed coffee mingles with the tantalizing scent of sizzling bacon, wafting through the air and beckoning everyone to wake up and gather around the table. For many families, this is the backdrop of a beloved tradition: the Big Sunday Breakfast. It is more than a meal; it is a cherished ritual that brings loved ones together to celebrate food, conversation, and connection.

The Ritual of Preparation

As the clock strikes eight, the kitchen transforms into a bustling hub of activity. Family members drift in and out, each one contributing to the culinary symphony. The eggs crack between laughter, the pancakes flip with a soft thud, and the biscuits rise in the oven, creating a comforting rhythm that sets the tone for the day. There's a sense of anticipation in the air, a joyous energy that fills the room as everyone pitches in.

Even the youngest family members have a role to play. Little hands can whisk together batter or set the table with colorful plates and cutlery. These small tasks build a sense of ownership and pride that makes breakfast feel like a joint achievement. The act of preparing food becomes a bonding experience, fostering not only culinary skills but also family unity.

The Spread

When the meal is finally laid out, it is nothing short of a feast—a celebration of flavors and textures that caters to everyone's taste. The table is adorned with a colorful array of dishes: golden brown pancakes stacked high, fluffy scrambled eggs seasoned to perfection, crispy bacon, and sautéed vegetables that add a splash of color. Fresh fruits provide a refreshing contrast, while homemade jams sit invitingly beside crusty bread rolls.

For some families, the spread includes regional specialties or cultural dishes that reflect their heritage. Be it a spicy shakshuka, ever-popular huevos rancheros, or a classic British fry-up, these meals tell stories of tradition and memory, making breakfast a journey through the family's culinary history.

With Stories
LEARNING ENGLISH

Bonding Over Breakfast

As the family gathers around the table, laughter and conversation flow as freely as the syrup on the pancakes. It's a time for everyone to reconnect, share stories from the week, discuss plans for the upcoming days, or simply enjoy the comfort of each other's company. This shared meal often becomes a sacred space where worries fade and joy abounds, reinforcing family bonds.

In a fast-paced world where weekday mornings often feel rushed and chaotic, the Big Sunday Breakfast serves as a gentle reminder to slow down and savor the moment. It's an opportunity to pause, reflect, and appreciate not just the food but also the people who surround you.

Children learn the value of togetherness and the importance of nurturing relationships, while adults rediscover the joy of connection through simple yet meaningful interactions.

Creating Lasting Memories

Over the years, the Big Sunday Breakfast becomes more than just a meal; it evolves into a repository of memories. Stories of children growing up, milestones celebrated, and loved ones lost find their way into these breakfasts, adding layers of meaning to the gathering. Special occasions, such as birthdays or anniversaries, often culminate in elaborate breakfast spreads, solidifying their significance in the family lore.

As new generations come into play, traditions may evolve, but the essence remains the same. Children become parents, and they carry forth the spirit of the Big Sunday Breakfast, adding their own twists and flavors while honoring the legacy of family meals passed down through the years.

With Stories
LEARNING ENGLISH

The Legacy Continues

In an age where technology often prevails over human interaction, the Big Sunday Breakfast stands as a testament to the power of communal dining. Whether it's a simple gathering of two or a sprawling brunch with extended family, the essence of connection remains. It serves as a weekly reminder that, while the world may change around us, the warmth of shared meals and cherished moments will always hold a special place in our hearts.

As you prepare for your next Sunday breakfast, consider how you can add your unique touch to this timeless tradition. Experiment with new recipes, invite friends to join, or perhaps even create a themed breakfast that reflects your family's current interests. The possibilities are endless, but one thing is certain: the Big Sunday Breakfast will remain a feast not just for the body, but for the soul—a celebration of life, love, and the bonds that tie us all together. So, gather your loved ones, roll up your sleeves, and embrace the joy of Sunday mornings together.

In an age where technology often prevails over human interaction, the concept of the Big Sunday Breakfast stands as a powerful testament to the enduring importance of communal dining. This weekly ritual offers an opportunity for connection that transcends the hustle and bustle of our increasingly digital lives. Whether it's a simple gathering of just two individuals catching up over coffee and pancakes or a sprawling brunch filled with laughter and stories shared among extended family members, the essence of connection and togetherness remains at the heart of this tradition.

The Big Sunday Breakfast serves as a poignant reminder that, while the world around us continues to evolve at a dizzying pace—filled with distractions from screens and notifications—the warmth generated from shared meals and cherished moments will always hold a uniquely special place in our hearts. It is in these gatherings that we find solace, support, and a sense of belonging, all nurtured by the act of breaking bread together.

With Stories
LEARNING ENGLISH

As you prepare for your next Sunday breakfast, take a moment to reflect on how you can infuse your unique perspective and creativity into this cherished tradition. Why not experiment with new recipes, stepping outside your culinary comfort zone to discover new flavors and techniques? Consider extending your invitation list to include friends or neighbors who might otherwise spend their Sunday mornings alone. You might even think about creating a themed breakfast that mirrors your family's current interests or passions, whether that be a cultural cuisine, a seasonal celebration, or even a nostalgic nod to favorite childhood dishes.

The possibilities for enhancing your Sunday breakfast experience are truly endless, limited only by your imagination and willingness to explore. Yet, amidst all of these different variations and innovations, one thing remains certain: the Big Sunday Breakfast is destined to be a feast not just for the body but for the soul. It becomes a vibrant celebration of life, love, and the indelible bonds that tie us all together. So, as the sun rises on another Sunday morning, gather your loved ones, roll up your sleeves, and embrace the joy that comes from sharing a meal together. Create an atmosphere filled with laughter, conversation, and warmth, allowing the shared experience of breakfast to strengthen your connections and foster a sense of community that can last long after the last plate has been cleared. By nurturing these moments, you not only honor the tradition of the Big Sunday

Breakfast but also enrich your own life and the lives of those around you.

With Stories
LEARNING ENGLISH

Tom and Julia's Breakfast Escapade

Sundays have always held a special place in the hearts of Tom and Julia. For them, it's more than just a day of rest; it's an opportunity to embark on a culinary adventure that sets the tone for the week ahead. This particular Sunday promised to be no different, as they planned to explore new flavors, experiment with ingredients, and perhaps even share a few laughs along the way.

The Perfect Start

Bright sunlight streamed through the kitchen window, illuminating the space and creating a cozy atmosphere. Tom, with his penchant for savory dishes, had his heart set on creating a classic eggs Benedict with a twist. Julia, on the other hand, had been inspired by a recent food blog she had perused, and was eager to whip up fluffy banana pancakes adorned with a generous dollop of whipped cream and fresh berries.

"Why don't we make it more interesting and have a little friendly competition?" Julia suggested, her eyes twinkling with mischief. "We can each showcase our breakfast masterpiece and let our taste buds decide who won!"

Tom chuckled, recalling their earlier breakfast battles, and readily agreed. "Bring it on! May the best chef win!"

Culinary Showdown

With their culinary competition in place, they set to work. Tom cracked the eggs with precision, expertly poaching them in a simmering pot of water. He whipped up a rich and creamy hollandaise sauce, infusing it with a hint of lemon for a zesty kick. Meanwhile, Julia looked on, giggling as Tom's serious demeanor contrasted with the excitement bubbling within her.

With Stories
LEARNING ENGLISH

Julia, in her corner, mashed ripe bananas into a rich batter, blending in flour, milk, and a touch of vanilla. The scent of sweet banana wafted through the kitchen, causing Tom to momentarily pause and take in the delightful aroma. He glanced over, a smile playing on his lips, "That smells fantastic! But can it compete with the deliciousness of my eggs Benedict?"

"You'll have to taste it to find out!" Julia retorted playfully, her determination unwavering.

The Taste Test

After what felt like an eternity of sizzling pans and whirring whisks, both dishes were finally plated. Tom presented his eggs Benedict in a way that could easily grace the cover of a food magazine—the perfectly poached eggs glistened atop toasted English muffins, drizzled with hollandaise sauce and garnished with a sprig of parsley. Julia's banana pancakes, stacked high and adorned with vibrant berries and a fluffy cloud of whipped cream, looked like a whimsical masterpiece. The moment of truth arrived as they sat down to taste each other's creations.

They took their first bites simultaneously, savoring the flavors. Tom's eyes widened in delight as the creamy hollandaise complemented the runny egg yolk, while the crisp muffin soaked in the sauce added layers of texture and taste. Julia beamed, her pancakes melting in her mouth with the warmth of banana coupled with the sweetness of honey and the tartness of fresh berries.

"Okay, I'll admit," Tom conceded with a grin, "these pancakes are giving me a run for my money!"

With Stories
LEARNING ENGLISH

The Great Debate

After a second helping and some playful banter, they took a moment to reflect. While they both had their favorites, they realized that there was no need for a winner. The real adventure lay in the memories they had created together, the spirited competition sparking joy in their hearts.

"Next week, we should try making something completely different," Julia suggested. "How about homemade bagels or an elaborate omelette?"

"I love that idea! The possibilities are endless." Tom responded, already excited about their next culinary venture.

Conclusion

With laughter echoing through their kitchen and their plates wiped clean, the Sunday breakfast adventure of Tom and Julia had once again proven that food can be more than just a meal. It's a celebration of creativity, teamwork, and friendship. As they cleaned up the remnants of their delightful feast, they looked forward to what challenges and flavors the next sunday would bring.

In a world that often rushes by, this little tradition of theirs had become a cherished ritual, a beacon of connection, warmth, and endless adventure—a reminder that sometimes the best journeys begin right at home.

With Stories
LEARNING ENGLISH

Two Boys and Their Basketball Adventure

On a crisp winter evening, anticipation hung in the air as the sun dipped below the horizon, bathing the city in hues of orange and purple. Two boys, Jamie and Ethan, were bubbling with excitement. They had been counting down the days to this moment—the basketball match featuring their favorite team, the Blue Hawks, at the local arena.

The Build-Up

Jamie, a slender kid with a mop of curly hair, was the more outgoing of the two. He had been a die-hard Blue Hawks fan since he could remember, donning his team jersey with pride. Ethan, on the other hand, was quieter, often content to sit back and observe rather than jump into the fray. Yet, his passion for basketball matched Jamie's as they spent countless afternoons shooting hoops at the local park.

As they walked to the arena, their conversation was a symphony of enthusiasm. They discussed their favorite players—Jamie idolized the sharpshooting guard, Liz Turner, while Ethan admired the towering presence of center, Marcus Lee. "Did you see his last game? He had four blocks!" Ethan exclaimed, his eyes gleaming with admiration.

The boys arrived at the stadium, the energy palpable as fans streamed through the gates, each step resonating with the thumping bass of the pre-game music. Jamie and Ethan exchanged wide-eyed glances, their hearts racing as they joined the throngs of supporters clad in blue and white.

Inside the Arena

Once inside, the sight was overwhelming. The arena was a sea of blue, adorned with banners and flags, and the scent of popcorn and hot dogs wafted through the air. Ethereal lights danced above them, illuminating the gleaming hardwood court that was about to witness the clash of titans.

With Stories
LEARNING ENGLISH

They found their seats among the raucous crowd; they were just a few rows from the action. As the players warmed up, Jamie and Ethan cheered, trying to catch a glimpse of their idols. "Look!" Jamie pointed excitedly as Liz Turner executed a flawless three-pointer during warm-ups. The crowd erupted with cheers, and the boys could hardly contain their joy.

The Game Unfolds

Finally, the game began. The arena buzzed with energy as the referee's whistle pierced the air, signaling the start of the match. The Blue Hawks raced onto the court, and the cheer of the crowd reached a deafening crescendo. Jamie and Ethan stood up, hopping with excitement as they chanted their team's name, "Let's go Hawks!"

The first half of the game was a rollercoaster ride. The teams were evenly matched, each trading baskets in a back-and-forth display of athleticism. Liz Turner was dazzling, hitting shot after shot, while Marcus Lee dominated the paint with rebounds and powerful dunks. The boys were on the edge of their seats, each made basket igniting their enthusiasm.

Half-time arrived, and the boys took a moment to catch their breath. They discussed the standout plays and shared their hopes for the second half. "If Liz can keep this up, we'll definitely win," Jamie said confidently, while Ethan agreed, "And if Marcus continues to defend like that, they won't stand a chance."

The Thrilling Conclusion

As the second half kicked off, the tension mounted. With only a few minutes left on the clock, the score was tied. The arena was a mix of suspense and excitement, with fans on the edge of their seats. Jamie and Ethan held their breath as the Blue Hawks' coach called a timeout, strategizing for the final moments of the game.

With Stories
LEARNING ENGLISH

When the game resumed, it was a battle of wills. The clock ticked down. In the last seconds, the ball found its way to Liz Turner. Jamie and Ethan screamed in unison as she dribbled past defenders, weaving her way to the three-point line. Time seemed to slow as she released the ball in a stunning arc toward the basket.

Swish! The crowd erupted in jubilation as the ball sailed through the net, giving the Blue Hawks the lead. The boys jumped up, hugging each other in exhilaration, their voices rising above the roar of the arena. The final buzzer sounded, and the Blue Hawks emerged victorious.

The Aftermath

As the crowd began to disperse, Jamie and Ethan lingered, soaking in the atmosphere. They knew they had witnessed something special that night—a thrilling game filled with unforgettable moments. The exhilaration of the victory bonded them even tighter as friends.

On their walk home, they talked animatedly about their dreams of becoming basketball stars, sharing visions of dribbling down the court, and hitting game-winning shots in front of roaring crowds. The night had ignited their imaginations, cementing a shared passion that would carry them through many more games and adventures to come.

That chilly evening, amidst the wave of celebration and camaraderie, two boys found more than just a thrilling basketball match—they discovered the thrill of friendship and the power of dreams ignited by the love of the game.

With Stories
LEARNING ENGLISH

As the crowd began to disperse in waves of laughter and excitement, Jamie and Ethan lingered just a little longer, soaking in the electric atmosphere that surrounded them. The echoes of the final buzzer, the cheers of jubilation, and the rhythmic thumping of feet on the hardwood floor still reverberated in their minds. They exchanged wide grins, fully aware that they had just witnessed something exceptional that night—a thrilling basketball game filled with unforgettable moments that would forever be etched in their memories. The exhilaration of the hard-fought victory not only boosted their spirits but also bonded them even tighter as friends, creating an unbreakable connection in the aftermath of the triumph.

As they strolled home under the crisp night sky, the chill in the air only heightened their excitement and energy. Their conversation flowed effortlessly, animated and lively, as they exchanged thoughts and dreams about their aspirations of becoming basketball stars. They painted vivid pictures in each other's minds of themselves dribbling skillfully down the court, weaving through defenders, and sinking awe-inspiring, game-winning shots in front of roaring crowds. Each word fueled their enthusiasm, igniting their imaginations and solidifying a shared passion for the game that they both cherished. Hours melted away as they walked, the world around them fading into the background, and in that moment, it felt like nothing was out of reach. The night had sparked a fire within their hearts that would pave the way for many more games, adventures, and challenges they would face together in the future.

With Stories
LEARNING ENGLISH

That chilly evening, amidst the joyful wave of celebration and the camaraderie that enveloped them, two boys discovered something deeper than just a thrilling basketball match—they found the profound thrill of friendship united by shared aspirations and the powerful dreams that coursed through their veins, ignited by their love of the game. In that moment, they realized they were not just fans of basketball; they were dreamers with visions of greatness, ready to chase after their goals side by side, fueled by the magic of that extraordinary night.

Hours melted away as they walked, the world around them gradually fading into the background like a distant memory. The vibrant sounds of the city, the bustling streets, and the fading day all seemed to dim as their minds became entwined in thoughts of possibility and shared dreams. In that enchanting moment, it felt as if nothing was out of reach; the restrictions of reality blurred, replaced by a landscape where ambition knew no bounds. The night had sparked an exhilarating fire within their hearts, illuminating a path that promised the thrill of many more games, adventures, and challenges they would bravely face together in the future.

On that chilly evening, the air crisp with the promise of adventure, they found themselves immersed in a joyful wave of celebration. Surrounded by the camaraderie of newfound friends and familiar faces, the atmosphere buzzed with excitement and laughter, forming a blanket of warmth that enveloped them. Yet, for those two boys, the experience went beyond just the thrills of a basketball match; it blossomed into something far deeper. They discovered the profound thrill of friendship—an unbreakable bond forged through shared aspirations and the powerful dreams that coursed through their veins, ignited by their unwavering love of the game.

With Stories
LEARNING ENGLISH

In those precious moments, with the lights of the court sparkling like stars against the velvety night sky, they shared their visions and dreams, their voices filled with enthusiasm. They realized that they were not merely fans of basketball; they were dreamers, united with aspirations of greatness. Each dribble and shot made palpable their determination to succeed, to overcome every obstacle in their path. Ready to chase after their goals side by side, they felt an exhilarating rush of hope and motivation, fueled by the magic of that extraordinary night.

The bond they formed was more than just the play of a game; it was a partnership that held the promise of countless adventures ahead. In that fleeting yet unforgettable time, they understood that the power of friendship and shared dreams would propel them into a future brimming with potential, a journey that they would navigate together with unwavering spirit and boundless enthusiasm. With each step they took, they were carving out a legacy, one that would be marked by triumphs, lessons learned, and memories that would last a lifetime.

With Stories
LEARNING ENGLISH

A Heart in Pieces: A Boy's Unraveling Moment in a Café

In the bustling world of urban life, cafés often serve as an inviting sanctuary—an escape from the noise, a pause among the chaos. For one young man, however, a seemingly ordinary visit to his favorite café turned into a moment that would forever alter his perception of love and trust.

Eighteen-year-old Jake had always found solace in the corner booth of "The Cozy Nook," a local café adorned with warm wooden accents, fragrant coffee, and friendly faces. It was a place that housed countless memories of laughter and study sessions with his girlfriend, Lily. They often shared this intimate space, reveling in the comfort of one another's presence, surrounded by the aroma of freshly brewed coffee. Little did Jake know that this café would soon become a backdrop for heartbreak.

On a particularly gray Tuesday afternoon, Jake entered the café, his heart light with anticipation. He planned to surprise Lily with her favorite caramel latte, hoping to discuss their upcoming weekend getaway. As he approached the counter, he scanned the room, searching for her familiar smile. Instead, his world came crashing down as his heart sank—there across the room, sitting at a table meant for two, was Lily, laughing and leaning closely towards another man.

Jake felt the room spin as disbelief flooded his mind. He squinted, hoping the figure next to her would fade away, that this was all a cruel figment of his imagination. The warmth of the café felt like ice as he fought against the urge to confront the situation. He stood frozen, feeling as though he were in some surreal nightmare where time stood still. Was it a harmless meeting, or had he been betrayed by the one person he trusted most?

With Stories
LEARNING ENGLISH

The stranger beside Lily appeared to be older, exuding an air of confidence that only deepened Jake's insecurity. Their laughter echoed painfully in his ears, and each shared glance felt like a dagger piercing through the happy memories they had created together. Overwhelmed by emotions, Jake's mind raced with questions. Had Lily been dishonest with him all along? Was this the beginning of an end he never saw coming?

Conflicting emotions surged within him—anger, sadness, confusion. How could she? How could someone he adored capably create space for another man right before his very eyes? The jealousy clawed at him, whispering thoughts of inadequacy. He always prided himself on being supportive and understanding, but in that moment, all of that felt pointless and misplaced.

Unable to bear the sight any longer, Jake turned on his heel, abandoning his plans for the caramel latte. He stepped out of the café into the crisp air, still holding the door handle as if it could ground him in reality. The cold hit his face, yet he felt numb, drowning in a sea of heartbreak. For a moment, he considered confronting her, making sense of whatever was happening, but rage clouded his judgment. He felt the urge to escape, to insulate himself from the painful vision seared into his memory.

As he walked aimlessly through the streets, flashes of their relationship flickered in his mind. The countless moments of joy, shared hopes, dreams, and the deep connection they once had—all of it now seemed tainted. How could he reconcile the past with the haunting reality that unfolded before him?

Eventually, he found solace in the anonymity of a nearby park, where he could collect his thoughts. Sitting on a bench, the weight of his heartache pressed heavily against him. He engaged in an internal dialogue, grappling with the confusion spiraling within. Should he confront Lily and demand answers or simply walk away? Was it worth salvaging a relationship that could so easily be taken for granted?

With Stories
LEARNING ENGLISH

The sun began to set, painting the sky with hues of orange and purple, a stark contrast to the turmoil within him. The world continued to spin around him, indifferent to his suffering. In that moment, Jake discovered a profound realization—love, while beautiful, can also shatter just as easily. Trust, once broken, can lead to an insurmountable mountain of grief.

As the stars emerged, twinkling above like distant promises of hope, Jake made a choice. No matter the outcome, it was time for a conversation. It was time to open the door to honesty, to confront the feelings he had repressed. Whether it resulted in healing or closure, he owed it to himself to seek the truth.

The next day would mark the beginning of a new chapter, one where vulnerability and courage reigned over heartache. Jake had learned that sometimes, the paths of love lead us through the shadows before we can embrace the light.

As the fiery orb of the sun sank below the horizon, it cast a breathtaking kaleidoscope of colors across the sky, vibrant oranges blending seamlessly into deep purples, painting a masterpiece that signaled the end of the day. However, for Jake, this natural wonder was merely a backdrop to the emotional chaos swirling within him. The external world continued its relentless pace, people bustling about their lives, oblivious to the tempest of despair raging inside him. With every passing moment, he felt like an island of sorrow in an ocean of indifference, profoundly aware that while beauty surrounded him, his heart was heavy with the weight of unmet expectations and lost connections.

In that poignant twilight hour, a realization washed over Jake like a wave crashing upon the shore—the paradox of love. It could be a breathtaking experience, a feeling capable of illuminating even the darkest corners of one's soul, yet it bore the potential to crumble, to dismantle with a brutal swiftness that left destruction in its wake. The exquisite bond he once cherished had become tainted, trust frayed like an old thread, unraveling into a seemingly insurmountable mountain of heartache and grief. It was a harsh lesson, one that many learn too late: love, in all its splendor, comes with a vulnerability that can lead to profound sorrow.

With Stories
LEARNING ENGLISH

As the stars began to twinkle against the canvas of the night, serving as ethereal reminders of dreams and aspirations yet to be fulfilled, Jake felt a flicker of determination ignite within him. These distant points of light seemed to beckon him, whispering promises of hope and healing. He understood what he needed to do; it was time to summon his strength and engage in a conversation long overdue. No matter the potential outcomes that lay ahead, whether it was the mending of his wounded heart or simply the bittersweet taste of closure, he owed it to himself to boldly pursue the truth.

He resolved to open the door to honesty and vulnerability, knowing that embracing these elements would be crucial in navigating the complexities of his emotions. The next day loomed on the horizon, a blank slate filled with possibilities and uncertainties, yet brimming with the potential to breathe life into a new chapter. This chapter would be defined not by the remnants of his heartache, but rather by the courage to face his fears and express his true feelings. He had come to understand that journeys of love often meander through shadowy valleys before they can rise to the peaks of light and joy. With this newfound insight, Jake prepared himself to step into the unknown, ready to confront whatever lay ahead with an open heart and an unwavering spirit.

He resolved to open the door to honesty and vulnerability, recognizing that these two powerful elements would be absolutely crucial in navigating the intricate complexities of his emotions. In a world often dominated by fear and self-protection, he understood that it was only by allowing himself to be truly seen and understood that he could forge deeper, more meaningful connections with others. The next day loomed on the horizon, a blank slate filled with limitless possibilities and uncertainties, yet it became apparent to him that it was brimming with the potential to breathe life into an entirely new chapter of his existence.

With Stories
LEARNING ENGLISH

This upcoming chapter would be defined not by the lingering shadows of his past heartache, nor by the weight of regret that had once threatened to tether him down. Instead, it would be characterized by a newfound courage to confront his fears, to express his true feelings, and to embrace the raw authenticity of his being. No longer willing to let his past dictate his future, he had come to a profound understanding—a realization that the journeys of love and personal growth often meander through shadowy valleys. These valleys, while daunting, were essential experiences that could lead one to the enlightening peaks of light and joy that awaited on the other side.

With this newfound insight, Jake found himself invigorated and prepared to step into the unknown that the next day promised. He envisioned it as a canvas yet to be painted, each stroke representing a decision and each color emblematic of a feeling. He was aware that challenges lay ahead, yet he felt an unwavering sense of resolve to confront whatever lay in his path. Armed with an open heart and an unyielding spirit, he was ready to navigate the emotional landscape that awaited him, determined to embrace the highs and lows, and to trust that every experience would contribute to his growth.

As the dawn approached, illuminating the world with soft hues of hope, Jake took a deep breath, welcoming the light that signaled not just a new day, but a new opportunity—a chance to embark on a transformative journey fueled by honesty, vulnerability, and the tenacity of the human spirit.

With Stories
LEARNING ENGLISH

The Intersection of Care and Compassion: Exploring the Theme of Love in Doctor- Patient Relationships

In the realm of healthcare, the bond between doctors and patients often extends beyond mere professionalism. It dances on the fine line between care and compassion, revealing an intricate tapestry woven from experiences of vulnerability, trust, and the human condition. This article endeavors to explore the profound connection that can develop between doctors and patients, navigating the complexities of love in the context of illness.

Understanding the Doctor-Patient Relationship

At its core, the doctor-patient relationship is built on trust. Patients look to their healthcare providers for guidance, support, and healing during some of the most challenging times in their lives. This relationship, however, is not just transactional or clinical; it is deeply emotional. Patients often share their fears, hopes, and dreams with their doctors, revealing layers of their identity that remain hidden from others.

In many cases, this connection can lead to a form of love that transcends the usual boundaries of professional interaction. It may not always be romantic, but it can be characterized by deep empathy, understanding, and a shared journey toward healing. For some patients, a doctor's genuine care can make a critical difference in their emotional and physical recovery.

The Spectrum of Love in Healthcare

The love present in doctor-patient relationships can be categorized along a spectrum—from compassion and empathy to a more profound emotional connection.

With Stories
LEARNING ENGLISH

1. **Compassionate Care**: At the most basic level, doctors are trained to provide compassionate care. This involves acknowledging the patient's suffering and offering support and understanding. Studies have shown that patients who feel cared for are more likely to adhere to treatment plans and experience better health outcomes.
2. **Emotional Connection**: As the bond deepens, patients often feel an emotional connection with their doctors. This can manifest as mutual respect and admiration. It is not uncommon for patients to express gratitude that borders on affection, feeling that their doctors have not only healed their bodies but also touched their hearts.
3. **The Dangers of Overstepping Boundaries**: While emotional love can be beneficial in many ways, it also presents challenges. Doctors must navigate the delicate balance between providing emotional support and maintaining professional boundaries. Misinterpretations can lead to ethical dilemmas, misunderstandings, or even exploitation if not carefully managed.

The Impact of Illness on Love

Illness inherently brings with it a complexity that may amplify feelings of love, both positively and negatively. The vulnerability associated with being unwell often catalyzes strong emotions. In the face of illness, patients may experience existential fears that trigger profound connections with their healthcare providers.

1. **Mutual Recognition of Humanity**: Both doctors and patients are deeply impacted by the experience of health crises. For doctors, witnessing suffering can evoke empathy and compassion that transcends the clinical. For patients, recognizing their doctor as someone who has chosen to dedicate their life to healing can foster a deep sense of gratitude and trust.

With Stories
LEARNING ENGLISH

1. **Healing Through Love**: Many healthcare providers embrace the idea that love—whether as compassion, empathy, or genuine care—can be a powerful catalyst for healing. Patients who feel loved and supported are often more resilient, finding strength to face their challenges, which can lead to more favorable outcomes.
2. **Navigating Grief and Loss**: Illness can also bring loss, and the doctor-patient relationship can become a space for shared grief. Doctors invest emotionally in their patients, and when they lose a patient, it can weigh heavily on them. This shared experience of grief can deepen relational love, as both parties navigate the difficult waters of loss together.

The interplay of doctor and ill love reveals much about the human experience of vulnerability and connection. While the professional nature of the doctor-patient relationship imposes certain boundaries, the emotional currents that flow within it can create meaningful bonds. Ultimately, while love in the medical field may manifest in different forms, the underlying theme remains the same: genuine care and compassion can illuminate the path to healing, reminding us of our shared humanity in the face of illness. As we navigate the complexities of life, it is this love—fragile yet resilient—that can lead us toward hope and recovery.

With Stories
LEARNING ENGLISH

The Story of Doctor John and Emily

In the bustling corridors of St. Mary's Hospital, amidst the beeping monitors and soft whispers of nurses tending to patients, an extraordinary love story unfolded – the tale of Doctor John Roberts and Emily Parker. Both dedicated to their professions, they found in each other not just companionship but a profound connection that would redefine their lives.

The Meeting

John was a well-respected surgeon known for his expertise and unyielding commitment to his patients. Emily, on the other hand, was a compassionate nurse whose gentle demeanor often provided comfort to those in distress. Their paths crossed one fateful evening in the emergency room. John, in the midst of a complex surgery, called for additional support, and Emily rushed in, instantly showcasing her remarkable ability to handle pressure.

As they worked side by side, a spark ignited. They communicated effortlessly, navigating the chaos of the emergency room with an unspoken understanding that turned into mutual admiration. Hours passed as they focused on the task at hand, and by the time the last stitch was placed, both John and Emily knew this was only the beginning.

The Development of a Relationship

Over the weeks that followed, John's admiration for Emily blossomed into something deeper. He found himself looking forward to the moments they shared during shifts, the stolen glances across the bustling nursing station, and the quiet conversations during their coffee breaks. Emily, too, felt drawn to John's determination and passion for his work. What began as professional respect quickly evolved into playful banter and heartfelt exchanges, building a solid foundation for their relationship.

With Stories
LEARNING ENGLISH

It wasn't long before their coworkers began to notice the chemistry between them. Rumors of "Doctor Love" and the "Nightingale Nurse" filled the break room, often accompanied by knowing smiles and playful nudges. While they were both aware of the potential scrutiny, John and Emily chose to embrace their feelings openly. They planned casual lunches and began spending time together outside the hospital, discovering mutual interests in hiking, classic literature, and even cooking.

Challenges Along the Way

Despite the joy their relationship brought, the demands of their professions posed challenges. John faced long hours in the operating room, while Emily balanced multiple responsibilities on her nursing shifts. They found themselves stealing moments together, be it quick texts or late-night phone calls, always holding on to the hope of brighter days ahead.

One particularly challenging week tested their bond. An unexpected emergency surge had them both working overtime, leaving little time for each other. Frustrated by the lack of connection, Emily questioned if they could sustain their love amidst their hectic lives. However, John, determined to support her, made an effort to remind her of his feelings through small gestures – leaving surprise notes in her locker and planning an intimate picnic once their schedules aligned.

A Moment of Clarity

Finally, during one weekend when they could catch a break, John and Emily decided to go on a hike in the nearby mountains. As they reached a viewpoint overlooking a breathtaking sunset, they found themselves wrapped in the warmth of each other's presence. It was in this serene moment that Emily realized their love was worth fighting for.

With Stories
LEARNING ENGLISH

John articulated his feelings, expressing how their shared experiences only made him more certain of their connection.

With the sky painted in hues of orange and pink, they shared their dreams, fears, and future aspirations, solidifying their commitment to each other. That day, they promised to carve out time for one another amid their demanding careers.

A Love Story Transformed

As the months rolled on, John and Emily learned to navigate the complexities of both work and love. They established rituals – regular date nights, weekend getaways, and dedicated time for open communication about their workloads. Their relationship not only weathered the challenges but flourished, with the two becoming each other's anchors during the stormy seas of hospital life.

Their love became an inspiration to their colleagues, not just as healthcare professionals but also as individuals who cherished the balance between career and personal life. They became advocates for mental health awareness, emphasizing the importance of support systems in high-pressure environments like hospitals.

As the months rolled on, John and Emily gradually learned to navigate the intricate complexities of both their demanding careers and the precious bond they shared. At first, juggling the long hours of their jobs in the fast-paced hospital environment felt like an insurmountable challenge. However, as they settled into a rhythm, they discovered the value of establishing rituals that would serve as the foundation of their relationship. They initiated regular date nights, where they would escape from the pressures of work and enjoy time together, reconnecting over candlelit dinners or cozy movie nights at home.

With Stories
LEARNING ENGLISH

In addition to their date nights, they planned weekend getaways, little escapes meant to recharge and rejuvenate their spirits. Whether it was a spontaneous road trip to the mountains or a peaceful retreat by the lake, these mini-vacations provided them with the opportunity to step away from the chaos of hospital life and immerse themselves in each other's company, cultivating deeper intimacy and understanding. They also carved out dedicated time for open communication about their workloads, fostering an environment where they could discuss their feelings, worries, and triumphs without judgment. This practice not only strengthened their emotional connection but also allowed them to support one another during particularly tough shifts or stressful weeks.

Through their shared experiences and unwavering support, their relationship not only weathered the challenges of the healthcare field but began to truly flourish. John and Emily became each other's anchors, providing solace and reassurance during the stormy seas of hospital life. They found joy in small moments—sharing a cup of coffee before dawn, exchanging knowing smiles during hectic shifts, and celebrating each other's victories, both big and small.

Their love story became an inspiration to their colleagues, showcasing the delicate balance between career ambitions and a fulfilling personal life. John and Emily made it a mission to advocate for mental health awareness within their workplace, passionately highlighting the importance of having robust support systems in high-pressure environments like hospitals. They organized workshops and seminars focusing on stress management, resilience, and self-care, encouraging their peers to prioritize their well-being, just as they had learned to do.

With Stories
LEARNING ENGLISH

Through their proactive efforts, they inspired others to pursue not only professional excellence but also to cultivate meaningful relationships, underscoring that love and support could thrive even amidst the chaos of their demanding careers. Their journey together became a testament to the power of love, partnership, and mutual respect, proving that it is possible to find harmony and joy in both one's personal and professional life, even in the midst of the most challenging circumstances.

With Stories
LEARNING ENGLISH

The Unbreakable Bond: A Tribute to My Mom and Sisters

In a world often marked by chaos and uncertainty, there exists a sacred space within the heart of a family where love thrives unconditionally. For me, this space has been intricately woven by the unwavering love of my mother and the unbreakable bond I share with my sisters. Together, we embody the strength, laughter, and warmth that fill our home with life.

A Mother's Love: The Foundation of Our Lives

From my earliest memories, I can recall the soft melodies of my mother's lullabies that soothed me to sleep, wrapping me in her love as a cozy blanket. Throughout our childhood, she was our anchor, guiding us through the storms of life with her calming presence. Her laughter echoed through our home, infusing it with joy, while her gentle reassurances offered us comfort during challenging times. Mom was the force behind every family tradition, from holiday gatherings to casual Sunday dinners. She instilled in us the values of kindness, perseverance, and the importance of family. It was her unwavering belief in us that inspired us to reach for our dreams, turning our aspirations into realities. My sisters and I often joke that our mom has superpowers, the kind that can mend a broken heart or heal a scraped knee with just a kiss and a hug.

Sisterhood: A Journey of Love and Growth

Growing up with sisters brought a dynamic mix of camaraderie and rivalry, a beautiful dance between love and the occasional squabble. We shared everything, from clothes to secrets, each other's triumphs and heartaches. Those late-night conversations whispered beneath the covers, bubbling laughter over shared inside jokes, and the music of our lives blending into a beautiful symphony only we could understand.

With Stories
LEARNING ENGLISH

Though each of us is unique, our personalities complement one another in a way that strengthens our bond. Whether it was conquering school projects together or supporting one another through relationship struggles, my sisters became my confidantes, my staunchest supporters. In moments of despair, I found solace in their presence, and in moments of celebration, we became each other's biggest cheerleaders.

The Power of Forgiveness and Growth

Of course, no relationship is without its challenges. Sibling disagreements flared up occasionally, and it was in these moments that we initially felt distant. However, our mother's wise teachings on forgiveness and communication always pulled us back to what truly mattered. She encouraged us to voice our feelings, mend our differences, and always choose love. It was through these lessons that we learned to appreciate each other more profoundly, recognizing that our connection was worth fighting for.

As we transitioned into adulthood, our lives began to take different paths, yet our bond only grew stronger. We continued to support each other, celebrating milestones such as graduations, new jobs, and marriages. In the face of life's unpredictable turns, our sisterhood became a safe haven, reminding us that no matter where life took us, we would always share this sacred bond grounded in love—just as our mother had nurtured it.

A Reflection on Love and Legacy

Looking back, I realize how fortunate I am to have had a mother who was not just a parent but a guiding light, instilling in us the values of love, resilience, and togetherness. Her unwavering belief in us paved the way for a future filled with possibilities. And hand in hand with my sisters, I have the privilege of carrying on that legacy of love.

With Stories
LEARNING ENGLISH

As we gather with our mother to create new memories, my heart swells with gratitude. Each laugh we share and every embrace we give reminds me of the beautiful journey we've taken together. Amid the world's chaos, our family remains a sanctuary, an illustration of what love can achieve.

In the tapestry of life, our threads may be different, but woven together, they create a masterpiece. I am proud of the bond I share with my mother and sisters, a bond that reminds me daily that love, in all its forms, is truly the greatest gift of all.

With Stories
LEARNING ENGLISH

A Heartwarming Family Tradition

Family moments often shape who we are, teaching us values and creating cherished memories. One such memory that stands out for me is the time my sister and I spent washing clothes with our mother. It wasn't just about the chore itself; it was about the bonding, laughter, and lessons we learned along the way.

The Prelude: Setting the Stage

It was a sunny Saturday morning. The air was filled with the sweet scent of blooming flowers wafting in through the open windows. My sister and I were lounging around, enjoying a rare lazy weekend when my mother called out from the laundry room, her voice upbeat and inviting. "Ladies, it's time for some laundry duty!"

At first, we groaned in unison, trying to play the "I'm too busy" card. But our mother, ever the enthusiast for turning mundane chores into fun activities, had a different idea in mind. She promised us that this laundry session would be like no other; it would be a memorable adventure if we put our minds to it.

The Charm of Teamwork

As we gathered our supplies—a basket of clothes, bottles of detergent, and our favorite fabric softeners—my mother laid out the plan. "First things first, we'll sort our clothes by color, then we'll wash them together and maybe even dance a little while we're at it."

With Stories
LEARNING ENGLISH

Sorting the clothes became a game. My sister and I began competing to see who could spot the most mismatched socks or the brightest colored shirts. Our laughter echoed through the house, and soon we were twirling around, pretending to be laundry fairies casting spells of cleanliness on our clothes.

Mom joined in our antics, imitating our dances and adding in her signature moves that hadn't changed since the '80s - complete with dramatic spins and exaggerated arm gestures. It was a spectacle of familial love and silliness that could lift anyone's spirits.

The Art of Washing

Once the clothes were sorted, it was time to tackle the washing machine. My mother patiently explained how it worked. "Washing clothes isn't just about using soap and water; it's about knowing the right settings for different fabrics." We listened intently, absorbing every detail as she guided us through the buttons and dials.

As the washing machine hummed to life, we took turns pouring in the detergent, feeling a sense of accomplishment with each scoop. The rhythmic sound of the machine became a backdrop for our conversations, where we shared stories, dreams, and our hopes for the future.

Lessons Learned

While washing clothes might seem like a trivial task to an outsider, it became a perfect metaphor for life's lessons. My mother used this opportunity to share wisdom about teamwork and responsibility. She emphasized how, just like in life, sometimes things get messy, but with a bit of effort and cooperation, we can always clean it up and make everything right again.

With Stories
LEARNING ENGLISH

By the time we got to the rinse cycle, my sister and I had not only washed a cartload of clothes, but we had also washed away any sibling rivalries. For that brief moment, there were no arguments or disagreements—just the joy of being together.

Celebrating the Result

As the last load finished, we proudly hung up our clean clothes on the line outside to dry in the fresh breeze. The sight of our neatly hung garments fluttering in the wind symbolized the fruits of our labor and a job well done.

Afterwards, we all gathered in the kitchen, where my mother treated us with homemade lemonade and cookies. Sitting there, enjoying our refreshments, I reflected on how a simple chore had transformed into a beautiful bonding experience.

Conclusion: Cherished Memories

Looking back, those afternoons spent washing clothes with my mother and sister were more than just about cleanliness; they were about connection. They were about laughter, learning, and the loving bonds that keep a family together.

Now, whenever I tackle the chore of laundry, I fondly remember those days, and I realize that it's never just about getting it done. It's about creating memories and celebrating the little moments that make life so special. In our fast-paced world, it's these simple experiences that often hold the most meaning, and I cherish them fiercely.

With Stories
LEARNING ENGLISH

Looking back on my childhood, those afternoons spent washing clothes with my mother and sister were much more than a mere chore focused on cleanliness; they emerged as treasured experiences woven deeply into the fabric of our family life. Each scrub of the fabric and every splash of water was an opportunity for connection and shared laughter, where the mundane transformed into something magical. It was during those leisurely hours that we exchanged stories and insights, fostering a sense of learning that extended beyond the practicality of laundry.

As we stood together, sorting whites from colors and debating the best way to tackle stubborn stains, we created a rhythm that reflected our familial bond. The gentle hum of the washing machine became background music to our giggles and playful banter, and the scent of freshly laundered clothes filled the air like a comforting embrace, reminding us of home and togetherness. Those moments were about more than just the task at hand; they were about nurturing love, solidarity, and the understanding that we could depend on each other.

Fast forward to the present day, and every time I tackle the ever-persistent chore of laundry, those cherished memories flood my mind. I can almost hear my sister's laughter and see my mother's patient smile as she taught us the nuances of fabric care. It strikes me profoundly that laundry is never simply about the end result of neatly folded garments or a clean wardrobe; it serves as a canvas for creating new memories. Each time I sort through the clothes, I am reminded that it is these moments of connection—these small yet significant rituals—that truly shape our lives.

In an age marked by relentless hustle and bustle, where time seems to escape us, it is these simple, shared experiences that often hold the most meaning. I find joy in the rhythms of daily life, as I cherish not just the act of washing clothes but the memories embedded within it.

Those afternoons of laughter and love are etched in my heart, a reminder to celebrate the little moments that, despite their simplicity, bring immeasurable joy and connection to our lives.

With Stories
LEARNING ENGLISH

Exploring the Joys of Hotel Stays with Kids

When it comes to family vacations, finding the perfect accommodation can make all the difference. As parents, we often seek destinations that offer both comfort and excitement for our children, while still allowing us to relax and unwind. Enter the world of kid-friendly hotels—places designed not just to host families, but to create unforgettable experiences. From epic pools to treasure hunts, a hotel stay can quickly turn into an adventure for the whole family.

Choosing the Right Hotel

The first step in having a memorable hotel adventure with kids is selecting the right hotel. Many establishments now cater specifically to families, offering amenities and activities tailored to younger guests. Look for hotels that feature:

1. **Family Suites**: These accommodations provide extra space, allowing kids to play without disturbing the adults. A separate sleeping area or living space can help maintain peace during those all-important nap times.
2. **Swimming Pools**: A pool can be a magical feature for kids of all ages. Choose hotels that boast kid-friendly water slides, shallow areas, or splash pads. Just a few hours of splashing around can transform into priceless memories!
3. **Kids' Clubs**: Some hotels offer supervised kids' clubs where children can partake in organized games, crafts, and activities while parents take a much-needed break. This not only keeps kids entertained but also allows parents to bond over a quiet dinner or explore nearby attractions.
4. **Dining Options**: Look for kid-friendly dining options. Whether it's a restaurant that offers a varied children's menu or special buffet nights, ensuring your little ones have meals

they will enjoy can make dining out a breeze.

With Stories
LEARNING ENGLISH

My Brother's Adventure at the Hotel

Recently, my brother decided to spend his day off at a hotel that boasted an expansive park on its premises. As an avid lover of nature and the outdoors, he was thrilled to take a break from the daily grind and immerse himself in a serene environment filled with lush greenery, vibrant flowers, and the sounds of chirping birds. What was meant to be a simple outing turned into an unforgettable adventure that he was eager to share with the family.

Exploring the Hotel Grounds

Upon arriving at the hotel, my brother was greeted by the charming sight of the park that sprawled across the property. The hotel itself was an architectural masterpiece, but it was the park that captured his imagination. With winding paths, towering trees, and quaint benches scattered throughout, it was the perfect place to recharge.

He took a moment to breathe in the fresh air, feeling the gentle breeze that rustled the leaves above. The park was alive with activity; families picnicking, children laughing, and couples strolling hand in hand. It was a vivid reminder of the simple joys of life.

A Whirl of Activities

As my brother wandered through the park, he stumbled upon various activities that piqued his interest. There was a small pond where guests were feeding the ducks, a playground echoing with the sounds of delighted children, and even a designated area for yoga and meditation.

With Stories
LEARNING ENGLISH

Feeling adventurous, he decided to rent a bicycle offered by the hotel. Biking through the park was exhilarating; he felt the wind against his face as he navigated the winding paths, stopping occasionally to capture the breathtaking scenery on his camera. The vibrant flowers, the playful squirrels, and the shimmering pond made for perfect photo opportunities.

Finding Peace in Nature

One of the highlights of his day was finding a quiet spot under a large oak tree, where he decided to take a break. Sitting on a bench with a book in hand, he felt completely at peace. The hustle and bustle of city life seemed worlds away, and he could finally unwind and lose himself in the pages of his favorite novel.

In this serene environment, he reflected on life, his dreams, and the importance of taking time for oneself. The park was not just a recreational space; it was an oasis for people seeking solace amidst the chaos of modern life.

A Culinary Treat

After a few hours of exploring, my brother's adventurous spirit was rewarded with a visit to the hotel's café, which overlooked the park. He treated himself to a refreshing smoothie and a delicious sandwich made with locally sourced ingredients. Sitting on the patio, he enjoyed his meal while gazing at the picturesque view around him. It was the perfect way to fuel up after an invigorating day of activities.

As the sun began to set, casting a golden hue over the park, my brother realized how much he needed this day of adventure and relaxation.

His visit to the hotel park had rekindled his love for nature and the outdoors, reminding him of the importance of balance in life. In a world filled with digital distractions and constant busyness, he found sanctuary in this lush haven.

With Stories
LEARNING ENGLISH

A Flower Girl Meets a Policeman

In a quaint coastal town where the waves danced gracefully against the shore and the sun painted the sky in hues of orange and pink, a young flower girl named Lily embarked on a day of adventure. Lily, a bright-eyed girl of seven, was known in her village for her enchanting floral arrangements and her infectious laughter. On this particular Saturday, she had decided to take her colorful bouquets to the beach, hoping to sell them to sunbathers and beachcombers.

As Lily skipped along the sandy path, her basket brimming with blooming daisies, sunflowers, and roses, she felt a rush of happiness. The salty breeze played with her hair, and the laughter of children filled the air. The beach was a canvas of joy, with families building sandcastles, surfers catching waves, and seagulls soaring overhead.

Upon arriving at the beach, Lily set up her little stall under the shade of a vibrant beach umbrella. As she arranged her flowers, she was filled with excitement, imagining the smiles her flowers would bring to those who passed by. But as she tried to catch the attention of passing beachgoers, she noticed something unusual—a group of children playing close to the water's edge had begun to drift farther away from their parents, their toys scattered on the sand.

Suddenly, a stern yet kind voice interrupted her thoughts. "Hey, kids! You shouldn't be so close to the water without your parents!" Lily turned to see a tall figure, dressed in a crisp blue uniform, walking toward the children. His badge glinted in the sunlight, making it clear that he was a policeman on patrol.

The policeman, Officer Jake, had a kind smile that quickly put the children at ease. He knelt down to their level and calmly explained the importance of staying safe at the beach. "The waves can be unpredictable, and it's always best to stay where your parents can see you," he advised. The children listened intently, clearly drawn to his gentle demeanor.

With Stories
LEARNING ENGLISH

As the officer ensured the safety of the children, Lily couldn't help but admire his dedication. She had always thought of policemen as figures of authority, but watching him interact with the kids made her see a new side of them—far more than just protectors; they were also friends to the community.

Feeling inspired, Lily decided to approach Officer Jake. With a shyness that only a flower girl could possess, she approached him and said, "Excuse me, sir! Would you like to buy some flowers?" She held out her basket, which was bursting with vibrant colors.

Officer Jake chuckled, kneeling down once again to inspect her flowers. "These are beautiful! You have quite the talent," he praised. "I'd love to buy some for my partner at the station. We could use a bit of color in the police car!"

With that, he placed an order for a few vibrant sunflowers and daisies, and Lily's eyes sparkled with delight as she wrapped them up carefully. "Thank you! I hope they make your partner smile," she said earnestly.

The conversation flowed easily as they chatted about their love for the beach and the importance of community. Lily shared her dreams of becoming a florist and how she enjoyed bringing cheer to others through her flower arrangements. In turn, Officer Jake talked about his commitment to protecting the community and how much he enjoyed being out on patrol, especially on sunny days like this.

After making the exchange, Officer Jake waved goodbye, promising to stop by again. He walked away, flowers in hand, a scatter of joy and appreciation lingering in the air.

The day passed with Lily selling her flowers to many appreciative beachgoers. She learned that the beach was not just a place for relaxation; it could also be a connection point for the community, where friendships bloomed like the flowers in her basket.

With Stories
LEARNING ENGLISH

As the sun began to set, casting a golden glow over the horizon, Lily packed away her remaining flowers. She felt a sense of fulfillment—not just from selling her blooms, but from having met someone like Officer Jake, who embodied kindness, responsibility, and community service.

That day at the beach taught Lily that even a simple encounter can lead to meaningful connections. And as she walked home, she couldn't help but dream about the next adventure, hopeful that it would be just as enchanting as meeting the policeman with a heart as warm as the summer sun.

As the sun began to dip below the horizon, casting a breathtaking golden glow across the sky, Lily gently packed away her remaining flowers, the vibrant colors still vivid against the warm backdrop of evening. The air was filled with the sweet scent of blooming petals and the sound of gentle waves lapping at the shore, creating a serene atmosphere that enveloped her as she worked. Each flower she tucked away brought a smile to her face, not only because they were a part of her livelihood but also as a reminder of the connections she had forged that day.

She felt a profound sense of fulfillment wash over her—not merely from selling her exquisite blooms to passersby, but from the unexpected encounter with Officer Jake, a man whose presence radiated kindness, responsibility, and a deep commitment to community service. His friendly demeanor had caught her off guard as he stopped by her stall, exchanging pleasantries and sharing stories that painted a picture of a life dedicated to helping others. It was his genuine interest in her work and his appreciation for her artistry that made their conversation stand out, leaving an indelible mark on her heart.

That day at the beach had taught Lily an invaluable lesson: even the simplest encounters can blossom into meaningful connections that enrich our lives in ways we could never anticipate.

With Stories
LEARNING ENGLISH

As she strolled home, the sun casting long shadows behind her, she found herself daydreaming about the endless possibilities that lay ahead. Each step felt lighter as she allowed her thoughts to wander to future adventures, her heart swelling with hope and curiosity. She envisioned experiences that could rival the enchantment of meeting the policeman—those with a spirit as warm and inviting as the summer sun itself.

With each passing moment, her anticipation grew, fueled by the belief that the world was full of surprises and delightful meetings waiting just around the corner. Lily couldn't help but imagine how wonderful it would be to encounter more individuals like Officer Jake—people who, through their compassion and dedication, could inspire her and perhaps touch her life in unimaginable ways. As the stars began to twinkle overhead, she realized that life was a tapestry woven of both ordinary days and extraordinary moments, and she was eager to embrace whatever came next.

With each passing moment, her anticipation grew, blossoming like a flower unfurling its petals to greet the sun. Each tick of the clock resonated with her heart, fueled by a deep-seated belief that the world was not just a collection of mundane sights and sounds, but a vast expanse brimming with surprises and delightful encounters waiting just around the corner. Lily's thoughts danced around the possibilities, painting vibrant pictures in her mind of what lay ahead.

She couldn't help but imagine how wonderful it would be to cross paths with more individuals like Officer Jake—people who exuded warmth and kindness, whose lives were characterized by a rare blend of compassion and dedication. It was through such individuals that she felt the potential to be inspired, to learn from their stories, and perhaps, to have her own life touched in ways she had never imagined.

With Stories
LEARNING ENGLISH

Each moment spent in the presence of someone like Jake ignited a flicker of hope within her—a hope that the world was not as chaotic and overwhelming as it sometimes seemed, but rather a place where kindness could flourish and connections could blossom.

As the stars began to twinkle overhead, dotting the indigo canvas of the night sky with shimmering lights, she felt a profound sense of clarity wash over her. In that moment, it struck her that life was a complex tapestry, intricately woven from the threads of both ordinary days and the extraordinary moments that punctuated them. Each encounter, each conversation, and every fleeting smile contributed to the richness of her experience.

With an exhilarating rush of enthusiasm, she took a deep breath, ready to embrace the uncertainty that lay ahead. She was eager to dive headfirst into the flow of life, open to whatever opportunities and challenges awaited her. Whatever came next, she was determined to approach it with an open heart and mind, ready to learn, grow, and perhaps even make a difference in the lives of others, just as those she admired had. The world was vast, and she felt emboldened by the thought that every twist and turn could lead to something remarkable. With an exhilarating rush of enthusiasm coursing through her veins, she paused for a moment to take a deep, deliberate breath, filling her lungs with the vibrant energy of possibility. It was a moment of quiet reflection amidst the noise of the world, as she prepared to embrace the uncertainty that lay ahead, that vast and unpredictable landscape filled with both promise and potential.

With Stories
LEARNING ENGLISH

With an eager heart, she was ready to dive headfirst into the flow of life, surrendering to its rhythm and allowing herself to be swept away by its currents. The idea of venturing into the unknown sparked a fire within her, one that burned bright with the anticipation of discovering new experiences, forging connections, and confronting whatever challenges might cross her path. She felt a profound sense of openness stirring within her—the readiness to accept whatever opportunities life had to offer, be they grand or seemingly trivial.

No matter what came next, she had made a resolute decision to welcome it with an open heart and an inquisitive mind. She envisioned herself navigating through whatever life threw her way, determined to learn, grow, and evolve with each new encounter. The prospect of making a difference in the lives of others excited her, inspiring her to reflect on the numerous individuals she admired—those who had made their marks on the world through their kindness, courage, and tenacity. She yearned to emulate their paths, to offer compassion and support to those around her, weaving her own story into the larger tapestry of humanity.

As she looked out at the world, she felt emboldened by the thought that the journey ahead was filled with infinite possibilities. Every twist and turn could lead to something remarkable, something that could ignite her passion or reshape her understanding of herself and her place in the universe. The vast expanse before her, with its myriad of paths and choices, stirred a sense of adventure deep within. With each step she took, she carried the unwavering belief that the future was not a predetermined script, but rather a canvas waiting for her unique brushstrokes, a journey waiting for her to fully experience its wonders and challenges alike.

With Stories
LEARNING ENGLISH

The Story of a Market Owner and His Youngest Customer

In the bustling heart of Elmwood, an unexpected friendship unfolded between a market owner and a small girl named Lila. This story unfolds in a vibrant corner store that had become the heartbeat of the neighborhood, where fresh produce, blooming flowers, and the aroma of baked goods filled the air. The market was owned by Mr. Patel, a kind and jovial man whose big heart was as noticeable as his warm, welcoming smile.

Lila was a spirited five-year-old with a wild mane of curly hair and sparkling blue eyes that brimmed with curiosity. Every Saturday morning, she would visit Mr. Patel's market with her mother, who would chat with the owner as she browsed the aisles. But Lila had her own mission every week—she loved helping Mr. Patel arrange the fruits and vegetables, turning her simple visits into little adventures filled with laughter and learning.

One bright Saturday, while her mother perused the aisles for ripe tomatoes and fresh basil, Lila walked up to the brightly colored produce section and greeted Mr. Patel. "Can we play a game?" she asked, her voice filled with excitement. Mr. Patel chuckled, his eyes twinkling with delight. "What kind of game do you have in mind, my dear?"

"Let's see who can stack the apples the highest!" Lila proposed, her small hands already reaching for the bright red apples on display. Mr. Patel chuckled heartily, bending down to her level, and agreed. They set to work, carefully balancing apples on top of one another, giggling as the towers swayed precariously.

With Stories
LEARNING ENGLISH

As they laughed and stacked, a small group of shoppers gathered around, bemused by the sight of the market owner and the little girl engrossed in a friendly competition. Lila, with her infectious laughter and boundless energy, lit up the atmosphere. Mr. Patel commented about the importance of local produce, and Lila chimed in, her innocent perspective turning a simple game into an educational experience for everyone.

"You see, everyone?" Lila said, gesturing to the apples, "These are healthy snacks! And they make you stronger!" Mr. Patel couldn't help but clap his hands in pride. It wasn't just the game; it was the way Lila effortlessly drew others into their joyous moment. The shoppers were not only entertained but also started discussing their favorite fruits and creative ways to incorporate them into their meals.

As the weeks turned into months, Lila became a regular fixture at the market. She didn't just visit for the fruits and vegetables; she brought a spirit of community and connection. Mr. Patel often shared stories about his childhood in India, teaching her about the cultural significance of different foods. In return, Lila would share her adventures from school and her dreams of becoming a doctor to help people.

One day, a severe storm hit Elmwood. The winds howled, and rain poured down in sheets. The market was quiet and forlorn, and Mr. Patel worried about the impact on his small business. Lila, hearing about the storm, decided to visit the market, bundled up in her raincoat and rubber boots. When she arrived, the sight of Mr. Patel, shoulders hunched in worry, tugged at her heart.

With Stories
LEARNING ENGLISH

"Mr. Patel, we can make it better!" she exclaimed, determined as ever. Inspired by Lila's enthusiasm, he took a deep breath and smiled. Together, they brainstormed ways to bring customers back to the market. They made colorful signs, crafted flyers, and even organized a mini-cooking class featuring seasonal produce to draw the community together.

When the storm subsided, the sun shone brightly over Elmwood, and the community responded to their efforts. People came flocking to Mr. Patel's market, eager to lend support. They participated in the cooking class, shared laughter, and rekindled their sense of community. It wasn't just a market anymore; it was a gathering place where friendships thrived and understanding blossomed.

Through this simple yet profound alliance, Lila and Mr. Patel taught the neighborhood an invaluable lesson: that community isn't just a place, but a connection—a connection nurtured through kindness, laughter, and cooperation. The small girl and the market owner became not only friends but partners in cultivating a sense of belonging that transformed Elmwood.

As the seasons changed and years rolled on, Lila grew, but she never forgot her time with Mr. Patel. Eventually, she became the heart of the market in her own right, championing local produce and fostering bonds just as Mr. Patel had done. Their story served as a lasting reminder that sometimes, the most beautiful friendships bloom in the most unexpected of places, bridging generations and creating legacies that reshape communities.

Through their simple yet profound alliance, Lila and Mr. Patel imparted an invaluable lesson to the neighborhood: community is not merely defined by a geographical location, but rather by the connections forged among its members—a connection that thrives and flourishes through acts of kindness, shared laughter, and collaborative efforts.

With Stories
LEARNING ENGLISH

The small girl and the market owner transcended the roles of merely being friends; they became partners in fostering a sense of belonging and unity that fundamentally transformed the fabric of Elmwood.

As the seasons gracefully changed and the years unfurled, Lila blossomed into her own individual, yet she retained vivid memories of her cherished time spent with Mr. Patel. Eventually, she emerged as the heart and soul of the market, passionately championing local produce and nurturing relationships within the community, just as Mr. Patel had done before her. Their story endured as a poignant reminder that the most beautiful friendships often bloom in the most unexpected places, effectively bridging generations, creating legacies, and reshaping the very essence of communities.

In this ever-evolving tapestry of human connection, Lila's journey from a wide-eyed child to an inspirational leader illustrated how ties forged through simple acts of generosity and understanding can ripple outward, touching countless lives. Indeed, her relationship with Mr. Patel transcended time, illustrating the timeless truth that relationships rooted in compassion and empathy can foster a culture of unity, resilience, and love within a community. Elmwood, shaped by their bond, reminded all its residents of the power of connection, encouraging everyone to engage in acts of kindness and to celebrate the diversity that made their neighborhood a vibrant tapestry of shared experiences and dreams.

With Stories
LEARNING ENGLISH

In this ever-evolving tapestry of human connection, Lila's journey unfolds as a remarkable narrative, illustrating the profound ways in which an individual can grow and transform through the simple yet powerful acts of generosity and understanding. From the innocent curiosity of her childhood, Lila matured into an inspirational leader, demonstrating how the ties we forge with others can create ripples that extend far beyond our immediate surroundings, ultimately touching countless lives in profound ways.

Lila's relationship with Mr. Patel served as a beacon of hope and wisdom, transcending the constraints of time and circumstance. Their bond embodied the timeless truth that relationships grounded in compassion and empathy can cultivate a culture of unity, resilience, and love within the fabric of a community. This connection not only enriched their lives but also served as a pivotal example for others, showing that the strength of our relationships defines the strength of our communities.

The town of Elmwood, profoundly shaped by the bond between Lila and Mr. Patel, became a living testament to the transformative power of connection. It reminded all its residents—young and old, newcomers and long-time dwellers—of the importance of engaging in acts of kindness, no matter how small. This spirit of generosity permeated the community, encouraging individuals to look beyond their differences and celebrate the rich diversity that contributed to making their neighborhood a vibrant tapestry of shared experiences, dreams, and hopes.

In Elmwood, the stories of individuals intertwined, creating a collective narrative filled with warmth and understanding. Each resident's unique background added a thread to the communal fabric, showcasing how varied perspectives and experiences could coexist harmoniously. Lila, now a guiding figure known for her wisdom and kindness, inspired others to take action, whether through volunteering, offering a listening ear, or simply sharing a meal with someone in need.

With Stories
LEARNING ENGLISH

As the seasons changed and the years passed, the lessons learned from Lila and Mr. Patel remained etched in the hearts of Elmwood's residents. They became living embodiments of the notion that genuine human connections can bring about meaningful change—not only in individual lives but across the entire community. Together, they fostered an environment where empathy thrived, where laughter echoed through the streets, and where each member was encouraged to dream big, fueled by the unwavering support and love of their neighbors.

In this way, Lila's journey and her enduring friendship with Mr. Patel resonated throughout Elmwood, creating a legacy of interconnectedness. It served as a reminder that in a world often divided, it is the bonds we forge—grounded in understanding, respect, and compassion—that can heal and unite us, paving the way for a future rich in love and harmony.

With Stories
LEARNING ENGLISH

A Little Girl's Adventure at Uncle Joe's Farm

It was a bright and sunny Saturday morning when little Emma, a curious and adventurous seven-year-old, packed her bag with shorts, a favorite sun hat, and her well-worn sneakers. Today was the day she had been eagerly waiting for—the day she would visit her Uncle Joe's farm! With her parents offering enthusiastic goodbyes, Emma hopped into the family car and off they drove, the excitement bubbling inside her.

After what felt like hours of winding roads and fields filled with wildflowers, they finally arrived at Uncle Joe's place. The unmistakable scent of fresh earth and hay greeted her as they stepped out of the car. Uncle Joe, a jovial man with a bushy beard and twinkling blue eyes, was leaning against the wooden fence, waving cheerfully. "Emma! There's my little buddy!" he called out, his voice warm and inviting. Emma ran toward her uncle, her pigtails bouncing, and engulfed him in a big hug. "What are we going to do today?" she asked, her eyes brimming with excitement.

"Well, how about we start with some chores?" Uncle Joe suggested playfully, winking at her. "I could use a little helper!" Emma clapped her hands in delight. Chores at the farm meant lots of adventures! First on the agenda was feeding the chickens. Uncle Joe led Emma to the chicken coop, a charming wooden structure painted in faded red. Inside, the clucking hens busily pecked around, oblivious to the little girl's presence. Uncle Joe handed Emma a small bucket filled with grains. "Here you go, sprinkle it on the ground!" he instructed.

With Stories
LEARNING ENGLISH

Emma giggled as she scattered the grains, watching chickens scuttle around her feet. She loved their fluffy feathers and curious pecking, and she couldn't help but laugh when one particularly bold hen waddled up to her, eyes bright and alert. "This one likes me, Uncle Joe!" she shouted, bending down to pet the hen who was now eyeing her curiously.

Next, Uncle Joe took Emma to the garden. Rows of colorful vegetables stood tall, their vibrant hues contrasting beautifully against the deep green leaves. "You're in for a treat! Today, we'll be picking tomatoes and green beans."

With her small hands, Emma carefully plucked the ripest tomatoes, marveling at their smooth, shiny texture. She felt a sense of accomplishment with each ripe fruit she filled her basket with.

Meanwhile, Uncle Joe explained the importance of caring for the plants and the joy of growing your own food. Every moment was filled with discovery, and Emma soaked up every bit of knowledge like a sponge.

After the hard work in the garden, it was time for a picnic! Uncle Joe spread a checkered blanket under the shade of a large oak tree, and they settled down to enjoy freshly made sandwiches, juicy watermelon, and refreshing lemonade. As they ate, Emma listened to Uncle Joe share stories from his childhood, of adventures through the fields and mischievous pranks on the barn animals.

Post-lunch activities led Emma to the pond nearby. Uncle Joe taught her how to skip stones across the water's surface. After a few attempts,

Emma finally got the technique right, sending a stone dancing across the pond. "Look! I did it!" she exclaimed, her face lighting up with joy.

With Stories
LEARNING ENGLISH

As the sun began to set, casting a golden hue over the farmland, Emma and Uncle Joe headed back to the barn. The evening was tranquil, filled with the sounds of crickets serenading the dusk and the gentle mooing of cows returning to their shelter. Uncle Joe showed Emma how to help with evening chores, brushing down the animals and ensuring they were cozy for the night.

Finally, as stars began to twinkle in the night sky, Emma snuggled in her sleeping bag in the guest room of the farmhouse, her heart full of joy. Today had been a whirlwind of excitement, hard work, and cherished moments with her beloved uncle. As she drifted off to sleep, she dreamed of chickens, tomatoes, and the happiest day she had spent on Uncle Joe's farm.

Visiting Uncle Joe's farm wasn't just about the fun adventures; it was about nurturing a love for nature, learning the value of hard work, and creating beautiful memories that Emma would carry with her forever. It had been a perfect day, and she couldn't wait for her next visit.

as the sun dipped below the horizon and the sky transformed into a vast canvas sprinkled with twinkling stars, Emma nestled deeper into her cozy sleeping bag in the inviting guest room of the quaint farmhouse. Surrounded by the rustic charm of her uncle's home, her heart brimmed with joy and contentment. The day had been nothing short of a whirlwind, bursting with excitement and energy, filled with hard work and the kind of cherished moments that seemed to stretch on forever. Each activity had been an adventure, a new lesson learned under the watchful eye of her beloved uncle.

As she slowly drifted off to sleep, lulled by the gentle sounds of crickets chirping outside her window, her mind began to weave together the threads of the day's experiences into a tapestry of dreams. In her slumber, she envisioned playful chickens pecking at the ground, vibrant red tomatoes glistening under the warm sun, and the laughter shared between her and Uncle Joe as they tended to the farm.

With Stories
LEARNING ENGLISH

Each image was a snapshot of the happiest day she could remember, filled with the taste of fresh produce and the smell of earth after the rain.

Visiting Uncle Joe's farm wasn't just about the exhilarating escapades; it was so much more profound than that. It represented a foundational journey into the heart of nature, a seed planted in her young mind that nurtured a deeper appreciation for the environment around her. She learned the importance of hard work, the satisfaction that comes from tending to the land, and the joy of witnessing the fruits of her labor—both literally and figuratively.

Every activity on the farm, whether it was feeding the animals, helping to harvest the garden, or simply walking along the sun-dappled paths, contributed to a growing sense of responsibility and connection to the earth. These experiences were not just fleeting moments; they were building blocks of character that Emma would carry with her long after she left the farmhouse.

As sleep enveloped her, she couldn't help but feel grateful for the extraordinary day she had just lived. It had been a perfect blend of hard work, laughter, and love, the kind of day that stayed with you long after the sun set and the stars came out. With a heart full of warmth and anticipation, she eagerly looked forward to her next visit, dreaming of all the new adventures and memories yet to be made on Uncle Joe's beloved farm.

With Stories
LEARNING ENGLISH

Exploring History and Art: Angel's Day at the Museum

On a crisp Saturday morning, Angel, a lively and inquisitive student, set out to the local museum with her sketchbook tucked under her arm and a heart full of excitement. The museum, a grand structure adorned with historical architecture, stood as a treasure trove of knowledge just waiting to be explored. It was not just a day off from her studies; it was a chance for Angel to immerse herself in the stories of the past and the beauty of art.

As she entered the museum, the cool, slightly dimmed interior wrapped around her like a comforting blanket. The scent of polished wood and aged paper filled the air, and educated whispers of fellow visitors created a harmonious backdrop to her adventure. The museum was hosting a special exhibit on ancient civilizations, and Angel was particularly excited to learn about cultures she had only read about in textbooks.

Her first stop was the Egyptian artifacts room. The moment she stepped inside, she was met with the sight of intricately carved sarcophagi and stunning jewelry adorned with precious stones. Angel's eyes widened with awe as she approached a golden mask of Tutankhamun displayed under protective glass. She felt as though she were being transported back in time to a world of pharaohs and pyramids. With her sketchbook in hand, she quickly began to draw the mask, carefully capturing the details of the glimmering gold and the intricately painted features. This was no ordinary homework assignment; it was a chance to connect with history in a personal way.

With Stories
LEARNING ENGLISH

Next, Angel ventured into the room dedicated to the Renaissance. Here, she was surrounded by masterpieces from artists like Leonardo da Vinci and Michelangelo. The colors seemed to dance on the canvas, each brushstroke telling a story of its own. She marveled at the sheer genius of the art and felt an overwhelming sense of inspiration. Finding a quiet corner, Angel took a moment to sit on a bench, letting her thoughts embrace the beauty that surrounded her. She began to sketch a portion of da Vinci's "Mona Lisa," fascinated by the enigmatic smile that had captivated viewers for centuries.

As she moved from exhibit to exhibit, Angel couldn't help but think about how art and history are intertwined. Each piece she encountered had its own narrative — stories of love, war, innovation, and human hardship that shaped the societies of the time. She made notes in her sketchbook, jotting down thoughts and reflections about the civilizations she'd learned about, hoping to convey these ideas through her own art one day.

After a few hours of exploring, Angel found herself in the museum café, where she took a much-needed break. As she sipped on her hot chocolate, she flipped through her sketchbook, admiring her drawings while thinking about how the museum had sparked new ideas and goals for her future. Perhaps she would study art history or become an artist herself, showcasing the elegance of cultures long gone. The world was full of possibilities.

Before heading home, Angel stopped by the museum's gift shop. Between the colorful postcards and books on ancient art, she picked out a small replica of a Roman sculpture, a token to remind her of her inspiring day. As she walked back towards the entrance, she felt grateful for the enriching experience, the kind that would fuel her creativity and academic pursuits.

With Stories
LEARNING ENGLISH

Angel left the museum with more than just sketches — she carried with her a renewed sense of curiosity and wonder about the world around her. The visit was a testament to the power of art and history as tools for learning, reminding her that, just like the artists and historians before her, she had the ability to shape stories through her own unique lens.

For Angel, this was not merely a visit to a museum; it was the beginning of a lifelong adventure filled with discovery, inspiration, and imagination. As she stepped into the daylight, she felt ready to continue her own journey, armed with the lessons of the past and the inspiration of the present.

Angel left the museum with more than just sketches — she carried with her a renewed sense of curiosity and wonder about the world around her. Each piece of art, each artifact she had encountered, resonated within her, igniting a spark of imagination that had lain dormant for far too long. The visit was not merely a passive experience; it was a transformative journey that served as a testament to the profound power of art and history as invaluable tools for learning. With each brushstroke and every story told through the exhibits, she was reminded of the timeless nature of creativity, the way it transcends boundaries and connects individuals across centuries. In the quiet corners of the museum, Angel found herself captivated by the narratives woven into the art, each a reflection of the human experience in all its complexity. It dawned on her that, just like the artists and historians before her, she too possessed the ability to shape stories through her own unique lens. She realized that every sketch she created could serve as a dialogue with the past and a conversation with the future, urging her to explore themes that mattered to her and share her perspective with the world.

With Stories
LEARNING ENGLISH

For Angel, this was not merely a visit to a museum; it was the beginning of a lifelong adventure filled with discovery, inspiration, and imagination. The vibrant colors and intricate details of the artworks lingered in her mind, beckoning her to delve deeper into her own creativity. The experience offered her a sense of belonging in a realm where stories are told not only through words but through visual expression and historical context.

As she stepped into the daylight, the world around her seemed to shimmer with possibility. The sounds of the city blended harmoniously with the echoes of inspiration from the museum, filling her with a sense of purpose. The lessons of the past now felt like guiding stars, illuminating the path ahead. Armed with newfound determination, Angel felt ready to continue her journey, eager to embrace the opportunities that lay before her. With a sketchbook in hand and an adventurous spirit, she would embark on expeditions into the realms of art, literature, and history, collecting experiences and insights that would further enrich her understanding of the world. The adventure was just beginning, and she was excited to see where it would take her.

As she stepped into the daylight, a cascade of warmth enveloped her, and the world around her seemed to shimmer with boundless possibility. The sun hung low in the sky, casting a golden hue across the bustling streets, where life thrived in a beautiful symphony of sounds. The distant honking of car horns mingled with the cheerful chatter of pedestrians, while the rhythmic clatter of bike wheels on pavement

created a lively backdrop. These sounds of the city blended harmoniously with the echoes of inspiration she had absorbed from the museum, lingering in her mind and filling her with a profound sense of purpose.
Every brushstroke and sculpture she had encountered whispered stories of creativity and passion, igniting a fire within her.

With Stories
LEARNING ENGLISH

The lessons of the past, encapsulated in the art and artifacts that surrounded her, now felt like guiding stars—celestial bodies illuminating the path ahead and beckoning her to explore the myriad facets of life waiting to be uncovered.
Armed with this newfound determination, Angel felt a surge of confidence coursing through her veins. The weight of her ambitions felt lighter now, and she was ready to continue her journey, fueled by an insatiable curiosity and a heart full of dreams. Eager to embrace the opportunities that lay before her, she made a silent promise to herself to pursue her passions fearlessly.
With a sketchbook in hand—its pages blank and bursting with potential—and an adventurous spirit guiding her, she would embark on expeditions into the vibrant realms of art, literature, and history.
Each corner of the city held the potential for discovery, and she envisioned herself wandering through galleries, diving into local libraries, and exploring historical sites that spoke of times long past. She would collect experiences and insights, weaving them into the

tapestry of her life, further enriching her understanding of the world around her.

This was not just a journey of external exploration, but an inward quest for self-discovery. Each encounter, each moment captured in her sketchbook, would serve as a stepping stone, helping her articulate her own voice within the vast expanse of human experience. The adventure was just beginning, and she could almost taste the excitement that crackled in the air. She was thrilled to see where it would take her, trusting that with every step forward, she would grow closer to the artist she aspired to become and the stories she was destined to share with the world.

With Stories
LEARNING ENGLISH

Learning English with Maya: Tom's Journey to Fluency
In a small town where diverse cultures converge, a young man named Tom embarked on a transformative journey to master the English language. Surrounded by a plethora of communication styles and dialects, Tom recognized the importance of English not only in his personal growth but also in his professional aspirations. The journey began when he met Maya, an enthusiastic language teacher known for her innovative and engaging methods of instruction.

The Beginning of a New Challenge
Tom had dabbled in learning English before, but he had never fully committed to achieving proficiency. He often struggled with grammar, vocabulary, and pronunciation. Recognizing these hurdles, he enrolled in Maya's language class, eager to turn his aspirations into reality. The classroom was a vibrant space filled with students from various backgrounds, each sharing their unique experiences and challenges in learning English. Maya fostered a warm, inclusive environment that encouraged participation and collaboration.

Maya's Unique Approach
Maya's teaching style was anything but traditional. She believed that language learning went beyond rote memorization and tedious drills. Instead, she incorporated multimedia tools, games, and real-world interactions into her lessons. For Tom, this was a refreshing change. He eagerly participated in role-playing exercises that simulated everyday conversations, which helped him build confidence in speaking.

Maya also emphasized the importance of contextual learning. Instead of learning vocabulary in isolation, Tom and his classmates were encouraged to engage with the language through storytelling, song lyrics, and even cooking recipes. This immersive approach allowed Tom to see the practical applications of the words and phrases he was learning.

With Stories
LEARNING ENGLISH

Building Confidence and Community

As the weeks passed, Tom began to notice significant improvements. While he initially felt shy about speaking, the supportive atmosphere created by Maya and his classmates helped him overcome his fears. Group discussions became a platform for him to express his thoughts and ideas, and he found himself more comfortable with each passing day.

Maya organized conversation clubs where students could practice speaking in a less formal setting. During these sessions, Tom mingled with classmates, sharing stories from their cultures while absorbing new ways of expressing his own. This sense of community not only fostered language proficiency but also built friendships that transcended language barriers.

Beyond the Classroom

Maya understood that learning a language entails more than just attending classes. She encouraged her students to immerse themselves in English outside the classroom. Tom took her advice to heart. He began watching English movies, listening to podcasts, and reading books tailored to his interests. These activities allowed him to reinforce what he learned in class, while also discovering the rich tapestry of English-speaking cultures.

Additionally, Maya introduced technology into their learning experience. Tom started using language learning apps, which provided him with engaging exercises that suited his learning pace. With Maya's guidance, Tom learned the importance of setting goals – both short-term and long-term – that kept him motivated and focused.

With Stories
LEARNING ENGLISH

Progress and Achievements

As time went on, the progress Tom made became apparent. His vocabulary expanded, his pronunciation improved, and he developed a keen understanding of English grammar. Perhaps most importantly, Tom gained the confidence to express himself in English, both in writing and in conversation.

Maya's influence stretched beyond the mechanics of language. She taught Tom to appreciate the nuances that come with mastering a new language – the idioms, humor, and cultural references that make communication rich and meaningful. With her support, Tom successfully completed an English proficiency test, a significant milestone in his journey.

Conclusion: A Lifelong Journey

Tom's journey to learn English with Maya was not just about acquiring a new skill; it was about personal growth, resilience, and community. Through the engaging methods and supportive environment that Maya provided, Tom found himself equipped with the tools necessary for effective communication in English.

As he looks to the future, Tom realizes that learning English is a lifelong journey. Inspired by Maya's teachings, he is excited to continue exploring the language, pursuing new opportunities, and connecting with people around the world. For Tom, the journey is not merely about learning a language; it's about understanding and embracing the diverse and interconnected world we live in.

Don't miss out!

Visit the website below and you can sign up to receive emails whenever cemal yazıcı publishes a new book. There's no charge and no obligation.

https://books2read.com/r/B-A-XLDEB-YVXIF

BOOKS 2 READ

Connecting independent readers to independent writers.

Also by cemal yazıcı

One night, One bar, One life
Gel İngilizce Konuşalım
Ufkun Ötesinde Ütopyayı Keşfetmek
Yellow Chickpea
The English Explorer
English Explorer Stories
English Between Lines
İngilizce Satır Araları 65
English Stories
English stories turkish
English dialogue diaries 1-2
English Dialogue Diaries 1 2
English Learning Stories Rocky Stone 1
English Learning Stories Rocky Stone 1
Learning English With Podcast
Learning English With Podcast
English Learning Stories A1 A2 level
English Learning Stories A1 A2 level
English for German speakers
English for German speakers
Deutsche Dialogtagebücher 1-2
Deutsche Geschichten Lesen, lernen genießen
Eine nacht, eine bar, ein leben
With Stories Learning English

About the Author

Cemal Yazıcı is committed to developing a series of storybooks specifically designed to aid English language learning. Each book is meticulously crafted, focusing on a variety of themes that resonate with readers of different ages and backgrounds. He created a series of English stories, workbooks and English practice books on English.